Grey-cheeked
Parakeets
and other Brotogeris

Grey-cheeked
Parakeets
and other Brotogeris

Robbie Harris

Frontis: Grey-cheeked Parakeet. Title page, top to bottom: Canary-winged, Golden-winged, and Cobalt-winged Parakeets.

Photographs by Fred Harris

*This book is dedicated
to my children,
Larry and Debra.*

Distributed in the UNITED STATES by T.F.H. Publications, Inc., 211 West Sylvan Avenue, Neptune City, NJ 07753; in CANADA by H & L Pet Supplies Inc., Kingston Crescent, Kitchener, Ontario N2B 2T6; Rolf C. Hagen Ltd., 3225 Sartel Street, Montreal 382 Quebec; in ENGLAND by T.F.H. Publications Limited, 4 K Park, Ascot, Berkshire SL5 7DS; in AUSTRALIA AND THE SOUTH PACIFIC T.F.H. (Australia) Pty. Ltd., Box 149, Brookvale 2100 N.S.W., Australia; in NE ZEALAND by Ross Haines & Son, Ltd., 18 Monmouth Street, Grey Lynn, Auckla 2 New Zealand; in SINGAPORE AND MALAYSIA by MPH Distributors (S) Pte., Lt 601 Sims Drive, # 03/07/21, Singapore 1438; in the PHILIPPINES by Bio-Resear 5 Lippay Street, San Lorenzo Village, Makati Rizal; in SOUTH AFRICA by Multip Pty. Ltd., 30 Turners Avenue, Durban 4001. Published by T.F.H. Publications I Manufactured in the United States of America by T.F.H. Publications, Inc.

Contents

Lifting its wings, an adult Grey-cheeked Parakeet *(Brotogeris pyrrhopterus)* shows the orange color underneath. This is the basis for the name "Orange-flanked" Parakeet. Note the blue on some of the wing feathers.

The wing length of a Grey-cheek averages 117 mm. (according to Forshaw), and the overall length is 20 cm. (8 in.). The average weight of the adults in my stock is 54 grams.

Acknowledgements

This book would have never been possible without all the helpfulness, understanding and encouragement from my wonderful parents, children (Larry and Debbie), family and friends.

A very special thanks to my long-time dear friend Frank Lanier of West Hollywood, California, who has helped me obtain a great many of my birds and has been a wonderful, trustworthy friend.

To my veterinarians, Robert Clipsham, Hannis L. Stoddard and Max E. Weiss, I would like to express my gratitude for their conscientious help and all the work they've done on my birds.

And last, but never least, many thanks to my brother Leonard (if he hadn't learned to hand-feed my baby birds, I would never be able to go away once in a great while for a vacation), and my son Larry, who also learned to hand-feed chicks.

Introduction

The Grey-cheeked Parakeet is just one of several species in the genus *Brotogeris*. The large numbers brought into U.S. quarantine stations yearly, now and in the past, is evidence of their popularity. For years the most frequently available species was the Orange-chinned Parakeet, which was known as the Bee Bee Parrot or the Tovi Parakeet. The Canary-winged Parakeet is another *Brotogeris* species that has come into the country regularly through the years, and sometimes small numbers of Tuis and the other species filter in. Today Orange-chins are not available as often as they used to be, and the name Bee Bee is often applied to other *Brotogeris* species.

Most young and adult birds of these species can be easily and quickly tamed. Their high intelligence has made these little parrots very popular as house pets. Once large numbers of Grey-cheeked Parakeets were imported to the U.S., they quickly surpassed the others in popularity. The Grey-cheek rapidly attained a nation-wide reputation as the finest pet bird available. The great majority of Grey-cheeks are sold as "sweet and naturally tame," and they really are very affectionate and intelligent birds. They are also very bold, and, even though they are only about eight inches long, they will still challenge another parrot twice or three times their size. Our pet Grey-cheeked Parakeet will chase a large parrot, or go right up to the other bird and take something if it wants it. Many learn to talk quite plainly. They become very attached to their owners, and there is no doubt that

Above: Orange-chinned chick, five weeks old. The bronze wing patch is already visible. Below: Unweaned *Brotogeris* chicks: the two in the foreground are Orange-chins, with a Cobalt-wing behind.

Adult Orange-chinned Parakeet *(B. jugularis).* The average weight of this species is 58 grams. Heavier than the Grey-cheek, it is shorter overall (18 cm., about 7 in.) and smaller in other dimensions as well.

they make excellent pets. Their chattering voices can become loud at times, but a bird kept singly as a pet is not usually noisy.

The voices of *Brotogeris* parakeets may all sound the same to us, but they don't to the birds. A friend of ours named Peter Hocking lives in Peru. He has a pet Tui Parakeet which is kept outdoors during the day in a cage that hangs on a tree limb. Noisy flocks of *Brotogeris* parakeets and other parrots often fly over his house. Most of these flocks provoke no reaction at all from Peter's pet Tui. But when a Tui flock or even a single Tui flies overhead, his pet starts to call frantically. There is no doubt that all of these species have their own calls, even if our ears cannot hear the difference, for each species knows its own kind. Peter also said that a great many people in Peru keep *Brotogeris* parakeets as pets, because many are tame and sweet, learn to talk, and become quite attached to their owners.

If importation is prohibited, the price of the Grey-cheeks and the other *Brotogeris* parakeets will soar. Making wonderful pets as they do, in popularity they will always outshine most other parakeets. They will be as precious as emeralds and, no matter the price, still be in great demand. Keep in mind that already some of the *Brotogeris* species which were readily available just a few short years ago are now very difficult to find. These birds should not be kept only as pets; they must also be bred to ensure a stock of birds when importation ceases.

My husband and I keep and breed a great many species of birds besides the *Brotogeris* parakeets, and we have always found these birds to be simply delightful little characters. This book deals with the care, maintenance, and breeding of the *Brotogeris* species. With so many people being so intrigued by these birds, I can only hope that they will be ambitious enough to set them up for breeding, to preserve these wonderful birds in captivity forever!

The Genus *Brotogeris*

Members of the genus *Brotogeris* are distributed from southern Mexico through central South America. These are small, solidly built birds ranging from seven to ten inches in length. In size they are very similar to the familiar lovebirds, though a little more on the slender side. *Brotogeris* parakeets have wedge-shaped tails of various lengths, quite short in some species, while others have longish ones. Their wings are long and pointed, which enables them to be very swift fliers.

Like so many other parrots, they are primarily green in color, but blue appears on the wings and tail feathers and often on the head. Many members of the genus have a contrasting color, yellow to orange, in a small area of their plumage, and in some the markings involve brownish shades. In all species except one—the Tui— the iris is a dark brown. The Tui also has a uniformly dark beak, but the beaks of the others are variably horn colored, sometimes with a dark tip. The beak is the main reason for grouping these species in the same genus. They have a distinctive profile, much different from a lovebird or a Budgerigar, for example.

Eighteen *Brotogeris* forms (subspecies) have been described. Some have a distinctive appearance and are found in accessible places, but others look very much alike and occur in areas where field study is difficult. Therefore, the relationships of some are quite clear-cut, but the treatment of others differs from book to book. The most recent studies group the *Brotogeris* forms into seven species, as follows.

In the subspecies *chiriri* of the Canary-winged Parakeet *(B. versicolorus)*, the lores are fully feathered, compared to *B. v. versicolorus*, and the overall shade of green is different. Average weight: 60 grams.

Brotogeris versicolorus versicolorus, the nominate subspecies, is slightly larger than *chiriri* and somewhat heavier, averaging 65 grams. Less thick feathering on the face gives it an "old" look.

Brotogeris jugularis, the **Orange-chinned Parakeet,** at one time was the best known *Brotogeris* species. Also known as the Tovi Parakeet or the Bee Bee Parrot, it is distinguished by a bright orange spot on the chin and a bronze color on the wing coverts, which becomes a brownish green on the back. The basic green of the body is lighter on the throat, breast, and abdomen. There is a large, bright yellow patch on the under wing coverts which can be seen only when the wing is lifted. The crown, lower back, rump, thighs, and underside of the tail are tinged with blue, while the flights show blue and green. The legs are a gray flesh color. Compared to the Grey-cheeked and Cobalt-winged parakeets, this seven-inch bird seems to have a disproportionately smaller head and a beak that is not so large and hooked. The range of *B. jugularis jugularis* extends from southwestern Mexico to northern Colombia and northern Venezuela.

B. jugularis exsul replaces the nominate form in eastern Colombia and western Venezuela. The smaller chin spot is a paler orange, and the blue tinge is missing from the thighs and the underside of the tail.

B. jugularis apurensis is no longer considered to be a separable subspecies.

Brotogeris cyanoptera, the **Cobalt-winged Parakeet,** also has an orange chin spot, but its forehead is a dull yellow, unlike the Orange-chin. The common name describes the wing flights and primary coverts, which have a bright blue. The central tail feathers also have blue, but the underside of the tail is a yellowish green. Only blue and green appear on the underside of the wing, which is another difference from the Orange-chin. On the crown and nape the green is tinged with blue, and on the back and wings it becomes almost olive. The upper mandible is horn colored, turning brownish toward the tip. The feet and legs are pink with a brownish tint.

One of the shorter-tailed species, this bird measures about seven and one-half inches. I have found with our pairs that the males are a little larger than the females, with slightly larger heads and beaks and a slightly brighter coloring. The young we raised resembled their parents. They are duller in color as they feather in, and the base of the upper mandible is a grayish color which fades quickly after a few months.

The nominate subspecies occurs in southern Venezuela, southeastern Colombia, northeastern Peru, eastern Ecuador, and northwestern Bolivia. Two other subspecies have been described from the edges of its range:

B. cyanoptera gustavi from Peru is duller and differs mainly in that it has the bend and edge of the wing yellow, and the yellow on the forehead is greenish.

B. cyanoptera beniensis from Bolivia is paler; it has yellow on the edge of the wing like *gustavi*, and on the primary coverts as well. Like *cyanoptera*, it has a yellow tinge on the forehead and lores, and blue on the crown and nape.

Brotogeris chrysopterus, the **Golden-winged Parakeet,** gets its name from its orange primary coverts. Its chin spot is an orange brown color, and its forehead band is dark brown. The blue tinge of the crown continues onto the cheeks, and, as usual, there is some blue in the flights. The underwing coverts are green. Overall, this species has the darkest shade of green, which is still darker on the wings and back. The feet and legs are a pale yellowish brown. At six and one-half inches, this is the shortest *Brotogeris* parakeet, also being short tailed.

B. chrysopterus chrysopterus is found in eastern Venezuela, the Guianas, and north of the Amazon in Brazil.

B. chrysopterus solimoensis is a separate population found only around Manaus, Brazil. It closely resembles

Because of the shade of yellow on the wing coverts, the species has the name Canary-winged Parakeet. In this sub-species, *chiriri*, only yellow appears in the wings, and the green is lighter overall.

The subspecies *B. v. versicolorus* has canary yellow in the wing and a large patch of white as well. Often, however, when the wings are folded, the white does not show. *Versicolorus* is a darker green.

chrysopterus, but with a reddish brown on the forehead and a yellowish brown on the chin.

B. *chrysopterus chrysosema* is the largest form, about eight inches long. It differs by having yellow primary coverts, and the yellowish orange of the forehead continues onto the lores. Its chin spot is orange. It is restricted to an area along the Rio Madeira in Brazil.

B. *chrysopterus tuipara* occurs south of the Amazon in Para and Maranhao, Brazil. Orange is the color of the narrow frontal band, chin spot, and primary coverts, and there is yellow on the sides of the tail.

B. *chrysopterus tenuifrons* is another isolated subspecies, from the Rio Negro area in northwestern Amazonas, Brazil. It is said to be very much like *tuipara,* except that the forehead band is very small and brownish.

Brotogeris sanctithomae, the **Tui Parakeet,** is also one of the smaller (seven inches), short-tailed members of the genus. The yellow of its forehead extends to the crown, so that the bird looks very much like a small version of the Yellow-crowned Amazon (*Amazona ochrocephala*). Its most distinctive feature is the chestnut-colored beak. The wing flights are a bluish green, with the blue brighter on the primary coverts. There is also a bluish tinge on the nape, cheeks, and underside of the wing flights. The wing coverts and the back are a bright green, with the head a slightly duller shade. On the breast, abdomen, under the wings and tail, and on the lower back, rump, and tail coverts the green becomes yellowish. The iris is a glowing golden color. The legs are a grayish brown.

B. *sanctithomae sanctithomae* is found in the Amazon Basin west of the Rio Madeira.

B. *sanctithomae takatsukasae* lives along the Amazon from its mouth west to the Rio Madeira. It differs from

20

the nominate subspecies by having a streak of yellow behind the eye.

The remaining *Brotogeris* species are larger, partly because of their longer tails.

Brotogeris tirica, the **Plain Parakeet,** is accurately named in that it is the least colorful. The overall green becomes yellowish on the crown, cheeks, flanks, and under the wings. The wing flights and the underside of the tail are blue, and there is a tinge of blue on the hindneck and mantle. The upper back and wing coverts have a brownish tinge. The legs are pink. A longish tail contributes to its nine-inch length.

The Plain Parakeet inhabits eastern Brazil from eastern Bahia to southern Goias. This species is rarely available and scarce in captivity in the U.S.

Brotogeris versicolorus is called the **Canary-winged Parakeet** because of the bright canary-yellow color of the secondary coverts. Except for a slight blue tinge on the primaries, the subspecies *B. versicolorus chiriri* is an apple green, slightly more yellow on the underparts. Its lores are fully feathered. The legs are pinkish gray. Four inches of this nine-inch bird are due to the long, pointed tail. *Chiriri* is widely distributed through eastern and southern Brazil and Bolivia, Paraguay, and northern Argentina.

B. versicolorus behni occurs in central and southern Bolivia. Slightly larger than *chiriri,* its plumage lacks the yellowish tinge, and the underside of its tail is a bluish green.

B. versicolorus versicolorus has a duller shade of yellow on the secondary coverts, but its most distinctive characteristic is the white on the inner primaries and the secondaries. This subspecies is known as the White-winged Parakeet. Most of the time when the wings are folded closed against the body, the white patch is not visible;

A pair of Cobalt-winged Parakeets (*B. cyanoptera*). The only real resemblance to the Orange-chin is the chin spot. Averaging 65 grams, the Cobalt-wing is heavier than the Orange-chin, but it has a more slender build.

The Golden-winged Parakeet *(B. chrysopterus)* at 16 cm. (6.5 in.) has the shortest length in the genus. Yet it is one of the heavier: this one weighs 62 grams.

only the yellow coverts are seen. *Versicolorus* has a more olive green than *chiriri*, and its head is darker. The outer primaries are a bluish green, and a tinge of blue is found on the forehead, around the eyes, and on the upper cheeks. The lores are sparsely feathered. *Versicolorus* is intermediate in size between *chiriri* and *behni*. It occurs to the north of the range of *chiriri*, in the Amazon Basin from Colombia, Ecuador, and Peru, east to the river's mouth.

Brotogeris pyrrhopterus, appropriately called the **Grey-cheeked Parakeet,** can be quickly distinguished from others of the genus by its gray forehead, cheeks, and chin. The large bright orange patch on the underwing coverts is the basis for its other names: Orangewinged, or Orange-flanked, Parakeet. When a bird is sitting on a perch with both wings held close against its body, the only orange color visible is a small amount just peeking over the tips of the shoulders. The primary coverts are blue, and the primaries are a greenish blue. The crown is bluish also. The rest of the body is green, a little paler on the underparts. The legs are pinkish. The Grey-cheeked Parakeet occupies a small range in western Ecuador and northwestern Peru.

Though it is unlikely that further study will change the classification of the *Brotogeris* forms very much, this is not impossible. What appears more likely is that it will have to be enlarged, for new species of birds are still being discovered in South America.

I have had the opportunity and pleasure to meet and speak with a man who may have seen a *Brotogeris* parakeet which has not yet been collected and described. This bird is the same size and shape as the Canarywinged Parakeet. It also has the same green color, but without the yellow wing patch; instead, a bright red covers the entire head. I was told the head color is similar to that of the Red-masked Conure. Peter Hocking spotted this bird many years ago while he was on a hunting expedition with some natives to the head waters of the Ucayali River near the border of Brazil, east of Pucallpa. A flock of them landed in a tree, and while he tried to shoot one with his .22 rifle, they flew off, but he got to see them quite well. Years later, he found that others too had seen flocks of these "Red-headed Parakeets" feeding in trees. They had been seen along the low mountain range which divides Peru from Brazil, only an hour's hike out of the town of Contamana. Later he spoke to someone who had seen a caged one, which the owners had raised after finding a nest. Unfortunately, he could never manage to find out who owned the pet. If this bird turns out to be another *Brotogeris* parakeet, I am left to wonder just how many more species are flying around that we are unaware of? I hope in the near future we will hear more about this "Red-headed Parakeet."

Hybrids and Mutations   Hybrids result when two different species of birds breed and produce young. Whether hybrids are fertile depends on how closely related the parent species are. Should the birds be quite different, as from different genera, then the hybrids would more than likely be sterile. Many times, of course, fertility varies among individuals. If hybrids are produced, it is best that they go for pets and not be used in breeding. If hybrids are repeatedly mated with pure birds, the result could be birds that would appear to be pure but in fact would not be. This means that if an unusually colored bird comes from a pair of birds that appear to be pure, it would be hard to determine whether it is the result of hybridization in the past or is a true mutation.

I have found reports of hybrids in *Brotogeris* dating back to the 1940s. A male Grey-cheeked Parakeet had been bred with a female Orange-chinned Parakeet and

Grey-cheeked Parakeets, a breeding pair. After surgical sexing, the female was banded on the left leg, the male on the right.

Tui Parakeets *(B. sanctithomae),* an adult pair. While other *Brotogeris* have dark eyes and a light beak, Tuis have a dark beak and striking golden irides. Their average weight is 58 grams.

produced one chick. A male Orange-chinned Parakeet and a female Plain Parakeet had a clutch of four eggs, of which three hatched. A male Orange-chinned Parakeet paired with a female White-winged Parakeet and hatched two hybrids from a clutch of six eggs; the first chick died almost immediately, and it was most unfortunate that the last surviving chick died suddenly when it was almost fully feathered. There have been many other reports of hybrids from pairings such as these. Back in 1917 an unusual pair of birds decided to set up housekeeping. The male was an Orange-chinned Parakeet and the hen was a Rose-ringed Parakeet (*Psittacula krameri*). Three eggs were laid by the hen, but despite their efforts to raise a family, none of the eggs were fertile.

Mutations have occurred in many *Brotogeris* species. A blue mutation occurred in the Plain Parakeet at the turn of the century in Budapest. Many offspring were reared, but the mutation was lost during World War I. Other reports of a blue mutation have more recently come from a Brazilian bird collection. Many years ago, a blue Orange-chinned Parakeet was spotted in a flock of wild birds (the orange chin spot was replaced with white). A white bird, which was believed to be a Tui Parakeet, has also been reported.

Selecting a Parakeet

Imported Birds   The large majority of Grey-cheeked and other *Brotogeris* parakeets which are offered for sale to the public by dealers and pet shops are imported, quarantined birds. These birds have been brought to the U.S., usually directly from South America, and placed directly into quarantine stations which are strictly controlled by the Department of the Interior. It is not unusual to have five thousand Grey-cheeks or other *Brotogeris* species in a single quarantine station. A plastic or metal numbered leg band is put on every bird for identification. If a bird dies, it must be carefully preserved, and an autopsy is performed to find out the exact cause of death. Government officers check the birds for a full thirty days to be sure they are all free from Newcastle disease, which is extremely deadly to poultry. As you may remember, many years back Newcastle disease was very disastrous for the poultry farmers. Thousands of chickens died or had to be destroyed because of this virus. Also, many parrots were killed by government agents at that time if there was any chance of their coming into contact at any time with the disease. This is the reason for the precautions being taken now, so history will not repeat itself. The strict thirty-day isolation, it's hoped, will prevent the spread of this serious disease.

But it's unfortunate that other bird diseases are not looked for at the same time. The Grey-cheeked Parakeets released from quarantine stations are usually in excellent health, but close surveillance for illness should still be

Handling a bird, to examine its health or for other reasons, reveals characteristics not easy to see otherwise. Orange is extensive on the underwing coverts of the Grey-cheek (above), while the orange patch on the Golden-wing (below) is fairly small.

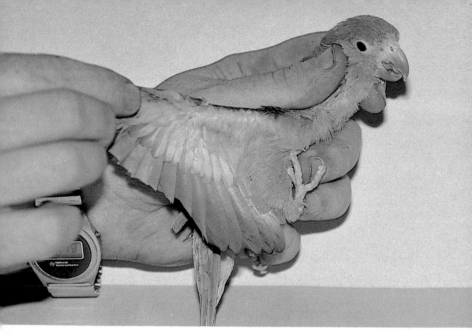

The underwing coverts of an adult Orange-chinned Parakeet (above) differ from those of a Grey-cheek in being more yellow. The Orange-chinned chick (below) shows another feature of the genus *Brotogeris:* young birds are colored like adults as soon as they feather in.

exercised, just as when purchasing any new bird. Remember, the only disease which would result in a shipment of Grey-cheeks or other parakeets not being released by the U.S. Government for sale would be Newcastle disease. The new bird should be watched and even checked by a vet, because there is always the possibility of other kinds of disorders. Just use common sense when it comes to purchasing a bird.

Birds released for sale after quarantine usually still have their leg bands. These bands usually fit tightly on the bird's leg. They may be removed by the owner at any time. A vet can do this for you easily, with a special band cutter. We have all the bands removed from our birds when we take them to our vet for surgical sexing or a checkup. We also keep a band cutter on hand in our house in case of an emergency. I have seen and heard of many unbelievable things happening to birds because of leg bands. If your bird has a leg band and you wish to leave it on, just keep a very close watch on the leg with the band. Dirt or a small seed can get under a fairly wide, tight-fitting leg band and irritate the leg. The leg will start to swell, and if the band is not removed immediately, it can cause the loss of the leg. I have seen bands slide up over the bend of the leg; this too will cause the leg to swell and become inflamed. I have purchased birds in this condition, where the leg was so swollen with pus and blood that there was no doubt that an infection had set in. I removed the band immediately and bathed the leg twice a day with a cotton ball dipped in hydrogen peroxide. Fortunately, this has worked for me every time, and soon the leg was as good as new.

There have been many pets that have hung themselves up by the band, on a toy or in their cage. If the bird is not freed in time, it could lose a leg or even die. I had a Grey-cheek on which the metal band was just slightly open. The bird was found hanging on the wire of the cage. It had been climbing around on the bars, and the small opening of the band hooked onto a cage bar. When the bird started to chew at the band, the opening turned further from the bar and made it impossible for the bird to get free. The more the bird struggled, the tighter the band got as the leg started to swell. I check my birds often during the day, and luckily I found this bird in time. The only loss was a bar from the cage. So just think about the things that could happen while you are away from home shopping, working, or on vacation; maybe a trip to the vet to remove the band before a problem occurs is a good idea.

Examining for Health   When purchasing a new bird it is very important that you give it a physical examination. This examination should include the body, eyes, head, face, nostrils, cere, mouth, beak, feathers, skin, feet, and legs. If at all possible, try to check the bird's droppings in the cage where it has been housed, to see if they are too watery. Very loose or watery droppings can be a sign that the bird is not in the best of health. When the bird is moved to a new cage, stress can cause the droppings to be watery for a while, simply because the bird is nervous. Also, you should observe the bird closely while it is still in the cage it is accustomed to. Stand back so you do not scare the bird, and check to see if the bird carries itself proudly and is not droopy or puffy.

Check the wing carriage and make sure the wings are held neatly folded. If one wing hangs down, this could mean that the wing may have been broken at some time and did not heal properly. The bird may not be able to fly, and in a large aviary being able to fly is a must. Breeding any bird that cannot fly must be done in a cage. If a bird unable to fly falls from high up in an aviary, it could prove fatal. I have found that most Grey-cheeked Parakeets recently released from quarantine have had their flight feathers clipped. This is done in order to keep them tame, since they enter the quarantine stations already tame. This procedure ensures that they remain gentle and do not become nervous and flighty. Other *Brotogeris* species, such as Canary-winged and Orange-chinned parakeets, generally are fully flighted, since they are usually not tame upon arrival in our country.

The eyes of any bird say quite a lot when it comes to health. They should appear bright and clear, not tearing, sleepy looking, or swollen. When you approach the cage, the bird should be very alert.

The feathers should look smooth, strong, and shiny. There should be no bare skin, gray down patches, twisted or badly broken feathers; if so, this could mean a vitamin deficiency, or the bird could be a feather plucker. Birds which have just come out of a quarantine station have gone through an awful lot. Some of them have ragged and rough-looking feathers, and some are even missing feathers from being plucked or from fighting with other birds, the result of temporarily over-crowded conditions. The feathers usually molt out after a few months, and generally the bird will look as good as new. I will admit that on occasion I myself have purchased a bird in very bad feather condition, but with much love and care and a proper diet the plumage has always returned to normal.

The feet should appear stable and the bird well balanced, grasping the perch securely. Check the feet and legs of the bird to see if they are free of any abscess, and make certain the bird does not limp from an injury, old or new. Loss of a toe or claw could have been the result of a fight. As long as the feet and legs look clean and there are no sores or swelling, the absence of a toe will have no bearing on the health of the bird. But if toes are swollen or curled, or if the skin on the foot pads or toes is cracked, this could come from a nutritional problem or unsanitary conditions; a bird in this condition should be avoided.

The cere should be clean, not wet or dirty from runny nostrils, which could mean a cold, an upper respiratory condition, or something even worse. Check for wheezing or rattling sounds, which could also indicate an illness. The beak should look strong and solid. If the mandibles are crossed or overgrown, they will probably have to be trimmed periodically.

Check the skin on the bird thoroughly, as it should look clean and smooth; not flaky, scaly, or peeling. Abnormal skin could mean the bird has mites, a vitamin deficiency, or could even be suffering from dehydration. Avoid any birds with wartlike lesions, scabs on their skin, or swollen joints, which could mean an infection or other type of disorder.

It is very important that the overall appearance of the bird is solid. The bird should be well fleshed and not have a sharp breastbone. The vent feathers should be clean, not soiled with droppings, which might indicate the bird is sick. The main thing in selecting a good, healthy bird is to use your good judgment. Do not just rush out and buy any bird; look the bird over carefully and make sure it looks healthy. Also, be sure this is the bird you want. With careful consideration and patience, the bird you select should prove to be a good pet or breeder for many years to come.

Choosing a Pet   Ninety percent of the Grey-cheeked Parakeets coming into the U.S. are already tame. The tame birds are generally babies or very young birds; the babies will still have a grayish area on their horn-colored beaks. There are conflicting explanations for the tameness of these birds. I have heard stories that the tiny babies are removed from their nests by natives in South America and are hand-reared. There have been quite a few occasions when Grey-cheeked Parakeets arrived at quarantine stations still too young to eat on their own. In these instances they were offered soft foods, in addition to being hand-fed for the first few weeks after their arrival. Others have said that almost all Grey-cheeked Parakeets are naturally tame, with a sweet disposition. Whichever is true, with the possibility that both are, these birds do enter our country unusually tame, which is not commonly the case with any other kinds of birds.

About six years ago my friend Frank Lanier received a phone call from a quarantine-station employee informing him that some "new" little parrots were at the station. He was told this was the first shipment to enter the quarantine stations in the U.S. in years. The birds, over a thousand of them, were called Grey-cheeked Parakeets, and all were tame. He "flew" down to the quaratine station and found that the story was true. As he stuck his bare hand in the cage to take one of the little parrots out, his arm was instantly covered with the tame creatures. He was so excited with the Grey-cheeked Parakeets that he purchased fifty of them, and each and every one was as sweet as could be. When he got home with the birds, he phoned and said we must come over to see these tame gems. Fred and I went to Frank's to see what all the commotion was about. It was true that all fifty were completely tame. Having no fear of humans they would climb all over us and, best of all, would not bite! We immediately purchased six of these birds from him. This was the first time that I had ever encountered these extraordinary little parrots, and I have been fascinated with them ever since that day.

When selecting a Grey-cheeked Parakeet for a pet, pick out the tamest, most outgoing, curious, sweet bird. If you have many to choose from, this could prove to be difficult, because I have found with most that one is as sweet as another. It is usually best to choose a young bird for a pet. Extremely young Grey-cheeked Parakeets have horn-colored beaks tinged with grey streaks, which quickly fade in a few months. Also, do not worry if the overall color is not vivid, for most young birds are duller in appearance than adults. The main basis for selecting a pet is the personality of the bird. After you make your selection, be sure to find out what the bird has been eating. Some young Grey-cheeks prefer soft food at first and are eating very little hard seed. A good diet to offer a baby Grey-cheek would be Purina Dog Chow and Monkey Chow moistened with drinking water and made into a mush. Bread, corn, apple, bananas, and soaked seed should also be given. A variety of dry seeds should be in the cage at all times. The baby will gradually start to eat seed as it gets older.

Without a doubt, you will find out what a wonderful little pet a Grey-cheeked Parakeet indeed makes. Just remember to pick out a healthy-looking bird with a good personality, and you should have a wonderful pet for many years to come.

Other members of the genus *Brotogeris* offered for sale are usually quarantine birds also. These, unfortunately, do not usually come into the U.S. already tame, like the Grey-cheeked Parakeet. But with just a little patience, after a short time of loving, training, and working with these birds, you will find they too become just as tame and sweet as the Grey-cheeked Parakeet. They will be excellent pets with wonderful personalities. Be sure to start with a healthy, alert bird.

Isolating New Birds   If you are purchasing a bird such as a Grey-cheeked Parakeet for a pet and you do not own any other birds, then it is not necessary to worry about quarantining the bird. But if you already own birds, especially breeding stock, it is vitally important to isolate all new, incoming birds before they are added to your collection. This even includes birds that have just been released from a quarantine station. They were only quarantined for Newcastle Disease, so they could be harboring or coming down with still another type of illness. This will usually show within thirty days from purchase, as it is brought out by the stress and trauma of being moved again to new surroundings. If the newly purchased bird was carrying a disease and was put together with your already established stock, it could end up to be a disaster. Unfortunately, there are some diseases that cannot be detected, and all we can do is isolate all new, incoming birds for a full thirty days and hope for the best. If any of the new birds die, an autopsy should be performed right away by the state lab or by a vet to see what was the cause of death.

New birds should be placed in an area where no other birds are being kept. It would be ideal to quarantine all new birds at a friend's or relative's house—where no other birds are kept, not even a pet bird—for about a month. Be sure to feed, water, and clean the cages of all new birds *after* all of your other pets and stock have been taken care of for the day. When all bird chores have been completed, then wash your hands thoroughly with soap and hot water. Diseases have been spread among animals by their own handlers, so strict sanitary measures must be taken.

I observe new birds very closely to make sure everything appears fine. If any bird acts or looks abnormal in any way, I have my vet check the bird immediately. Generally, a throat culture is done on the bird by the vet, and within forty-eight hours he will have results indicating whether the bird has an ailment. If so, the proper medicine can be prescribed in the correct dosage and administered to the ailing bird immediately. Most of our new birds are surgically sexed right after we first get them, and they also are checked for illness at this time.

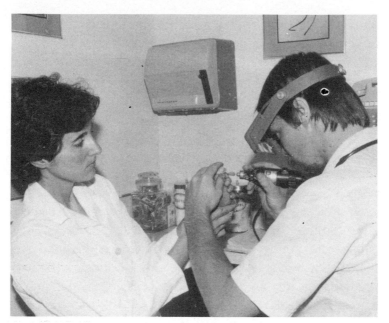

Dr. Hannis L. Stoddard III trims the overgrown beak of a Grey-cheeked Parakeet. The rotating stone grinds the beak back into shape.

This way we have an idea right from the start if the new birds are strong and healthy.

Generally, if you purchase a domestically bred baby bird from a breeder you know is very conscientious about the well-being of his birds, more than likely that bird will be quite healthy. New birds from other sources should be quarantined for thirty to forty-five days with a very watchful eye, since you do not know anything about the bird or its previous care or what it was exposed to.

Sexing Breeding Stock   It is almost impossible to visually determine the sex of a *Brotogeris* parakeet. These birds are not sexually dimorphic. In some cases the males will appear to have larger heads or beaks than the females, but more often this is not so. This could simply be one of the bird's individual characteristics, not a sexual trait. On occasion one can acquire small, petite males and large hens, as we have.

When we go to purchase pairs of birds and there are many to select from, we try to pick them out by the pelvic-bone method. We have had great success in obtaining mated pairs by this method in the larger parrots, such as conures, amazons, and even lovebirds, but it has proved to be more difficult to successfully select pairs of Grey-cheeked Parakeets and other *Brotogeris* species. This could be because the majority available for sale are babies and young, immature birds which do not have their pelvic bones set as yet. The pelvic bones are the two small bones just in front of the vent. Mature females usually have their pelvic bones set far apart so the eggs can pass between them. Males, on the other hand, have their pelvic bones very close together, with almost no space between the two. Also, many times a male's pelvic bones feel somewhat sharper to the touch than a hen's would. Again, the problem with this method is that immature *Brotogeris* do not have their pelvic bones set, making it very difficult to pick true pairs and very easy to make a wrong choice. Also, there is always an exception to every rule, and with some birds the pelvic-bone test just will not work, no matter how mature the bird is.

It would also be wrong to assume two birds are a pair just because they have developed what appears to be a pair bond, even if they are housed with many others in the same cage. These parakeets are very sociable birds and many times will continue to change companions, whether they are males or females. The only possible way that pairs will breed is to purchase at least six birds and set them up together in the same flight. At least four nest boxes should be installed, so that if they choose mates and develop pair bonds, they can select the nest

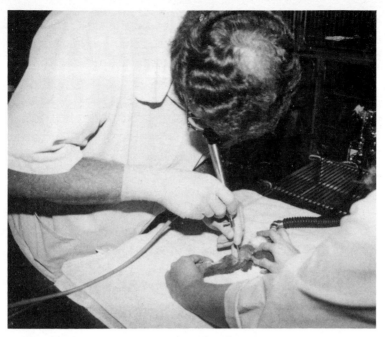

In the course of surgically sexing a Grey-cheek, Dr. Max E. Weiss is also able to assess its health.

box they want and go to nest. The birds that do not pair up could be removed, or the mated pairs could be set up in their own flights. I'll be honest and let you know that this method of pairing birds may not work. I once set up six birds in a flight. Instead of developing pair bonds, they became one big happy family. They would all eat, bathe, and play together. In the evening when it was time to retire for the night, they even roosted together in a small Budgie nest box. Needless to say, this method of pairing did not work for me!

The best and most accurate way to determine the sex of a *Brotogeris* parakeet is by surgical sexing. An experienced vet who specializes in birds performs this procedure on our birds. Surgical sexing is relatively simple for someone with the knowledge and the skill that comes from doing a lot of it. The birds usually come through just fine, and soon afterwards they are up again, as if nothing had happened. What is done is this: a small incision is made on one side of the bird, near the rib cage. An endoscope, or laparoscope, is inserted through the incision. The vet can then tell what sex the bird is, and often its approximate age and whether it is old enough to breed. The vet can also tell if the bird is in good health and is physically fit to breed.

We choose our parakeets first by the pelvic-bone method, followed by a look at head and beak shape, since sometimes the males have a little larger head structure. For example, both males in our two pairs of Cobalt-winged Parakeets have prominently larger heads than the hens. We also pick out the most colorful birds (bluer heads in the Grey-cheeked Parakeets), as this usually means they are older. Then, after we have made our purchase, we have the bird sexed surgically and also find out what state of health the bird is in. Using the pelvic-bone method and taking into consideration head and beak shape, followed with surgical sexing, has proved to be very successful for putting together *Brotogeris* pairs.

Keep one thing in mind: surgical sexing is an operation, and it can be a little more risky with the smaller birds like *Brotogeris*. So please find an experienced vet to perform this procedure, and do not be ashamed to ask your vet if he has done surgical sexing on these small parrots before.

Housing a Pet

Cages   Most Grey-cheeked Parakeets, as well as the other *Brotogeris* species, are notably active birds, which means they should have a fairly large cage to move around in. A cage which is suitable for a pet Cockatiel would do just fine for your *Brotogeris* parakeet. These little parrots love to climb about their cage, hanging upside down from the roof or just swinging on the swing. Any well-stocked pet store will usually have a large variety of cages to choose from.

Cages should be properly designed to make feeding and cleaning as easy as possible. Most well-built cages will have openings where feed cups slip in, so they can be removed easily for changing the seed and water. A cage for a Grey-cheeked Parakeet, for example, should have at least two cups; three is better. This way, one would be for water and two would be for different kinds of seeds: Budgerigar mix in one and sunflower seed in the other. Also, extra cups should be purchased for treats or fruits and vegetables. The cups should be washed at least every other day, thoroughly scrubbing under the rims, where food residue can build up. Drinking water must be changed daily; this includes scrubbing the water bowl out with soap to remove residue build-up and to prevent bacterial growth which could be harmful to your pet.

There should be a tray in the cage which can be quickly and easily pulled out for cleaning and for changing the soiled papers; this way, the cage door need not be opened. Otherwise, if there is no tray, seeds and other matter will be falling everywhere as you struggle to get the soiled paper out through the cage door. Also, if you decide to go on vacation and leave your pet with a friend who does not particularly care for birds, he will not have to struggle to keep the bird in its cage when he cleans the tray and changes the soiled paper. Old newspapers can be used in the tray of a cage. The older the paper the better, since the ink is considerably drier and will not come off on your birds' feet and feathers as it will from fresh newspaper. Cages with plastic seed guards on all four sides will help keep the seed hulls inside the cage, not on your floor. There are some sweet little pets that will insist on keeping their own cage clean by tossing out the hulls through the cage bars. A seed catcher that wraps around the bottom of the cage can be purchased at pet stores, and this will help catch any hulls and feathers tossed out or blown out when the bird uses its wings.

The cage bars should be spaced with about a half-inch between them—no wider. If the spacing is much wider, the bird could possibly get its head stuck between the bars while climbing and playing. At one time I myself had this happen to a pet bird. I was in the other room when, all of a sudden, our pet was screaming! As I ran into the room, I found him clinging to the side of his cage with his head caught between the cage bars. He could not release himself. I quickly spread the bars apart, and he freed his head. All I can say is, thank goodness I was home, or this could have been a very unhappy experience. Needless to say, he got a new cage!

Many cages come equipped with a metal grid which fits just above the tray. I have found that this grid is not necessary for Grey-cheeks and other *Brotogeris* parakeets. Most grids slide out easily and can be removed. Keeping the grid in place will only prevent your pet from walking in the tray and playing with its toys. These pet birds enjoy frolicking for amusement on the floor of the cage.

Be sure your pet's cage is not placed in a draft; for example, in front of a window or air conditioner, or next to or close to a refrigerator. Any of these could cause the bird to catch a cold, which could result in something even worse. Do not set up the bird cage too close to the ceiling, for heat rises. If a bird remains too warm for long periods at a time, this could cause the bird to molt out of season. If the room is about 68 F. where you are, it could be over 80 F. close to the ceiling. If you are in doubt about the height at which to place the cage, you should test the location. Put a thermometer where the cage is going to be placed and check the temperature several times during a full day. Take a temperature reading morning, afternoon, evening, and especially when the heater is on and when you are using the oven. This is an excellent way to see just how suitable this location will be for your bird's home.

If it is a nice day and you would like to place the cage in a sunny window, be sure there is a well-shaded area in the cage. This way, when the bird has had enough sun or gets too warm, it can retreat into the shade. This is necessary whether the house has air conditioning or not. I know of someone who left their pet locked in a cage in front of a closed window on a summer day. Half the cage had shade, and the house had central air conditioning. They left the house for the day, thinking their pet would enjoy looking out the window. As the day went on, the sun moved, shining in the entire cage. The bird died that evening from sunstroke, even though the house was 68 F. A bird can overheat from sunlight, even through a closed window. This was a very hard lesson for them to learn.

It is not necessary to cover your bird's cage at night. If the room is too cool or there is a draft, then the cage should be covered, but it would be best not to keep the bird in such conditions in the first place. Your pet will soon learn your routine and settle down to sleep when the lights go off. If you insist on covering the cage in the evening, be sure to leave a gap open on one side of the cage towards the wall. This will ensure that the bird has enough fresh air. Remember, once you start this practice, you cannot stop it until the weather becomes warm, as in the summer months. The bird will become accustomed to being covered, and should you forget to cover the cage one cool evening, your pet could end up catching a cold. So once you start, just be sure you cover the cage nightly.

If you decide to fix up a used cage, be sure to disinfect it thoroughly. You never know what state of health the previous tenant was in. If you are going to paint a cage, be sure the spray paint you use is lead-free.

Your bird's cage should be thoroughly cleaned at least once a week. This thorough cleaning would include scrubbing the feed and water containers in soapy water, and scraping the perches. The cage should also be washed, perhaps with a garden hose, and aired outdoors to dry. At this time the cage could be sprayed with a good bird-mite spray, which would help to prevent these little critters from becoming a nuisance to your pet.

Keep in mind that a cage is not supposed to be a prison, but instead a home. Your pet should be a companion, loved like any other kind of pet. You should allow the bird out of its cage periodically for play and exercise. This freedom from the cage will make for a more affectionate and happy pet.

Perches   It would be ideal for your pet's cage to have two or three perches inside, but this will depend on the style and size of the cage. You do not want to overcrowd the cage with perches; just make it more interesting for the bird to climb about by having perches at different levels. One perch should be placed in front of the seed and water cups, and a second up toward the top of the cage. You will find that usually the top perch is used for sleeping. Try to position the perches so your little friend's droppings will not fall into the feed cups. Also see if you can arrange them so the perches below will not become soiled when your pet is seated on the top perch. Be sure all the perches are tight fitting, as birds do not appreciate wobbly ones.

Cages are normally equipped with dowels which are one-half to three-quarters inch in diameter. A cage with perches too large or too small for your pet could cause foot problems. I have found that most Grey-cheeked Parakeets and their relatives enjoy tree branches immensely. These should vary in size from one-half to three-quarters inch in diameter. They seem to enjoy natural perches, since grasping them appears to be much easier. They also like to chew on them and peel off the bark, which is amusing for them and also helps to keep their beaks worn and in good condition, preventing overgrowth. You can replace one of the dowels that came with the cage or, if there is room, just add a tree branch. A branch of varying thickness is excellent for your bird, so do not worry about it being exactly the same diameter throughout its length. This way the bird can rest where it is most comfortable. Branches from fruit and willow trees make ideal perches. Just be sure that the branches have not been sprayed with insecticide or any kind of poison. Also be sure that the kind of tree you are using branches from is not itself poisonous. If you are not sure, check with your local plant nursery.

Perches and wooden swings can easily be cleaned by rubbing them with sandpaper. Clean off the sanded dirt and dust from the perches before placing them back in the cage, so the bird will not inhale the soiled powder. Never sand the perches while they are in your pet's cage. If you wash off the perches with water, do not put them back in the cage until they are completely dry, or your pet could catch a cold. If the perches must be put back immediately, you can use a hair dryer for a quick drying job.

Sandpaper perches or gravel covers which slip over the perches should never be used. They can do great damage to a bird's feet by causing calluses or soreness. How would you like to walk barefoot on stones all day?

Playgrounds   In addition to a cage, your pet ought to have a playground to climb and play on, to have some freedom out of its cage. Playgrounds, usually made of wood, can be purchased in most pet shops. There are various sizes and designs. One that is suitable for a Cockatiel will do fine for your Grey-cheeked or other *Brotogeris* parakeet. These playgrounds usually come with some feed cups, perches, a swing, and a ladder. If your pet has clipped wings, the playground should be easily accessible, being set up on top of its cage or nearby, so your pet can come and go to and from its cage on its own. You can have a few playgrounds throughout the house so your little friend can keep you company as you watch TV or do your work around the house. You can purchase an extralong ladder which leads from the playground to the floor. This way, if your clipped pet should become frightened and fall to the floor, it can quickly return up the ladder to the playground all by itself.

Keeping food, water, and an assortment of toys on the playground at all times will help to discourage your bird from wandering about the house. The bird will consider the playground its second home, enjoying itself as it exercises by swinging and climbing about outside of its cage, delighted with the freedom. Our pet Grey-cheeked Parakeet climbs to the top perch and exercises his wings by flapping as hard and fast as he can, as we wait for him to take off into the air one day, playground and all!

Remember, the playground is a play area, so your pet should not be left unsupervised for long periods of time.

You should not leave your bird on the playground if you leave the house. Your pet could stray off the playground and roam around. These birds are very intelligent creatures and, like people, do become bored. They are also very much like children, and if they know they should not do something, they'll do it anyway, especially to get attention. I used to leave my pets out on their playgrounds most of the day without the proper supervision. Many years ago, Dum Dum, our first pet Cockatiel, decided that round corners on our bedroom dresser were more satisfying to him than the pointed, square ones. So he proceeded to redesign the furniture, to my surprise. Another time, our pet parrot left his playground one day when I left the house. He proceeded to chew holes in Fred's leather boots. When I walked in the door, Rainbow had a guilty look written all over his face. I soon came across the boots, and Rainbow knew he'd had it now. That was the last time he was left out in the open when I was not at home. I still did not learn very much from this experience. Another day, Sunny, our little pet conure, decided my vase with blooming silk roses looked better with just the stems! I was right in the house when he proceeded to remove all the rose blossoms! Each of these times I was very lucky, as the damage was minimal. Unattended pet birds, however, may chew on drapes and other furnishings, doing quite a bit of damage. But, even worse, a bird could get hurt on something or consume something toxic and die. So please keep your eye on these curious little interior decorators!

Bathing   All our *Brotogeris* parakeets enjoy taking baths. Bathing keeps a bird well groomed and helps to keep it in good feather. If these birds are not provided with a fairly large bowl of clean water, they will just proceed to take a bath in their drinking receptacle. A small #1 ceramic or plastic bowl (five inches in diameter) can be purchased at your local pet store, or a similar bowl will do just fine. Some of your more shy and quiet birds will bathe by dunking their heads and beaks in the water and rubbing it over their bodies. But many will sit on the edge of the bowl, splashing water everywhere, soon jumping right in for real cleaning. If you are sitting next to the cage at this time, you too will get a shower! After bathing, many birds will sit for a time, cleaning and straightening each and every feather, placing each one in the right position. This helps to keep your pet looking neat and trim.

Some people spray their pet bird with clean, fresh water, to provide their bird with a shower. If you would like to find out if your pet would enjoy a spray bath, try it. Of course, this misting is done only in a warm house or on a summery day; otherwise you could end up giving your bird a cold. Pet shops and grocery stores carry small plastic bottles with a fine-mist sprayer. Wash and clean the bottle thoroughly before using it for your bird. Add clean, lukewarm water to the bottle. Mist your pet with just a small squirt or two at first, holding the bottle about twelve inches from the bird. Do this daily for about a week (again, only at warm temperatures). If by this time your pet catches the water with open wings and seems to beg for more, then this can be done as part of its daily routine. But if it tries to hide and moves as far from the mist as possible, you should discontinue the water spraying completely and let your pet take its bath when it wants to, by itself in a bowl of water. Remember, all birds have their own temperaments and know what they like and dislike.

Toys   Many different kinds of toys can be purchased at your local pet shop. Toys are designed to provide entertainment and exercise for your pet bird. Some of the toys you may find in a store will be a lava rock on a chain, bells, balls, a mirror, colored wooden sticks, and colorful balsa-wood rings. Be sure you examine the toy carefully before placing it in the cage with your bird. Some bird toys can be a source of potential harm to your pet. A bird can easily get hung up on a chain if it is wearing a split-type band that is slightly spread open (this band should be removed). Make sure any rings are either much smaller or much larger than your pet's head. If the ring is just a little bit smaller than your bird's head, it could get its head stuck in the ring while playing and then not be able to free itself. If your pet panics in this situation, it could end up a disaster. Also, be very wary of plastic toys. I know of a pet bird that chewed up and swallowed a piece of plastic from a toy and died. A necropsy done by a vet showed that the plastic tore up the intestines. So just be sure you use good judgment when selecting toys, making certain they are safe for your pet.

Most parrots, and especially *Brotogeris*, are very curious by nature and will examine any new object that has been placed in their cages. But some birds may be frightened by a new toy or any new article which looks strange to them. Do not force your pet to play with the toy if it is afraid of it. Just put the toy in the cage, be patient, and wait till your pet decides to investigate it. Should your bird avoid the new toy and that part of its cage for any great length of time, I would suggest that the toy be removed and tried another day. If your pet does not come to like the toy, try another kind of toy.

There are many objects around the house that will provide your pet hours of entertainment. Many of the best toys I have found are homemade and cost nothing! Nowadays everybody can use something for nothing, even your bird. Cardboard tubes from paper towels or toilet tissue can be great fun for your pet. These tubes can be cut into different sizes, with each size serving a different purpose. Your little pet can see through them, so a long one can be used for crawling through and hiding inside. Parakeets like to roll and chew on the tubes and carry and drag the small ones around their cage. Any size is just great fun for them to destroy! Wooden ice-cream sticks are also fun for them to carry around and chew on. An old iron or brass key can be hung from a chain or a piece of leather. Most pet birds find this most interesting, as they investigate the key with their little tongues and beaks. They will fling the key around on the chain, tug at the key, and even climb and swing on the chain. Just be sure the bird cannot get its toe or leg stuck in the links of the chain. Be sure to hang any toys such as this one away from the feed cups, not directly over them. You do not want the toy to interfere with your pet while it is eating or drinking. Here are a few more toys which usually can be found around the house: Nut shells, particularly from walnuts or almonds, provide an interestingly shaped object your pet will chew on and carry around. You can also crack a walnut in half, leaving the meat inside. This not only will be fun to play with, but is a great treat. Milk-Bone dog biscuits and rawhide dog bones or sticks are also fun for them to chew on. Empty wooden spools from thread, all wooden clothespins, or just plain pieces of wood in different shapes and sizes make good toys. You can drill some holes in the wood pieces to make it easier for your pet to pick them up with its beak and possibly even make them look more interesting. The list of potentially excellent and interesting toys could go on and on. Just look around the house, and see what you have in that junk drawer of yours. Maybe a large nut and bolt will turn out to be a fascinating plaything for your pet.

Feeders   There are various kinds of feeding receptacles which can be purchased and used for your bird.

Which feeders you decide to use will depend on the housing situation your bird or birds are set up in. A pet bird caged in the house will generally have different feeders from birds which are housed outdoors or set up for breeding. You will want to feed your bird in a way that is best for it and at the same time convenient and easy for you.

If your bird is a house pet, it is more than likely set up in a cage which already comes equipped with feed cups. I have found that three cups are quite adequate for Grey-cheeks and other *Brotogeris* parakeets: one cup for sunflower seed, one for Budgerigar mix, and the other for water. If your cage does not have enough cups, extra ones can be purchased at your local pet store. The cups used should be the larger size, as for Cockatiels. The small finch, Budgie, or treat cups will not be large enough to hold a sufficient amount of seed for these parakeets. I actually know of someone who starved their pet bird by using a single small treat cup for each day's ration of seed and another for water. Even filling that seed cup daily proved to be insufficient to keep the bird alive. Your pet should have large feed cups, so there will be food in front of the bird at all times.

There are also tube feeders available. I personally do not like these for Grey-cheeked parakeets or similar birds. I feel parrots like to look their food over and pick out what they like. Most tube feeders are too small for a Grey-cheeked Parakeet, which has a larger beak than a Budgie (for which these tubes were designed). The seed is not as accessible as it would be in a cup. Many birds insist on dumping all the seeds out of these tubes and onto the floor of the cage, so they can pick out the seeds they prefer and to make eating easier. These small tubes can hold only Budgerigar mix; any of the larger seeds can get stuck in the tube, and then your pet would not have access to food. Many of these tubes can also be used for water. This would be just fine, but remember that Grey-cheeked Parakeets like to take baths, so provide a cup or bowl of water along with the water tube.

If you are housing your birds in a large cage or aviary, there are various other feeders which can be useful. There are wooden or metal feeders divided by partitions, some having glass fronts, which can be particularly nice. With a glass front you can see at a glance when the birds are running low on seeds. Some of these feeders have three partitions, so sunflower, safflower, and Budgerigar mix can be put in different sections. This way, the birds eat the seeds they want without knocking out all the seeds while looking for certain ones. Most of these feeders will hold enough seed to last a pair of birds for about a week. I prefer metal feeders, as most *Brotogeris* species like to chew.

Metal rabbit feeders in all sizes are available at most feed stores. Three of the small feeders set up in a cage or aviary would be suitable, allowing the birds freedom to choose the seeds they want to eat without disturbing the seeds that are not wanted. Aluminum cake pans can be placed right under the rabbit feeders to catch hulls or uneaten seeds, in case the birds knock any out. Ceramic bowls (crocks) can also be used for seed. Crocks come in all sizes, and holders can be purchased so they can be hung on the sides of the cage or aviary. You can set up crocks to offer a different kind of seed in each one. Some pet stores even have heavy plastic bowls, which are also nice and will not break readily if dropped.

Feed your birds in the way most convenient for them and for the type of set-up you have. Feeders are not suited to some pairs of birds because they like to empty out all the seeds as a pastime before they eat any. For these birds, I suggest bowls for feeding. The main thing is that you feed your birds in the way that is best for both you and them.

Nutrition and Feeding

A Good Diet   It is very important that your bird receives a well-balanced diet. A properly nourished pet will be healthy, robust, and strong and can have the ability to resist most kinds of infections. An improper diet can result in vitamin deficiencies that lower the bird's natural immunities that it has toward many diseases. A well-balanced diet should include a fresh assortment of dry seeds, green food, fruits and vegetables, and fresh, clean water daily. These fresh nutriments contain the essential vitamins and minerals needed in your bird's daily diet and should keep your pet strong and healthy for many years to come.

Dry Seed   A pet Grey-cheek, or any other *Brotogeris* parakeet, must have an assortment of seeds available at all times. This can be a Cockatiel mix which most pet shops have, or different kinds of seeds can be placed in separate cups. Our pet has one cup with sunflower seed, one with a good Budgerigar mix (containing at least 40% canary seed), and a third with safflower seed. By feeding your pet in this cafeteria style, it can choose which seeds it wants to eat when it is hungry. This way, when you are replenishing its feed cups, there will be less waste, as you fill only the feed cups which need filling. Otherwise, for example, if your bird had Cockatiel mix in a cup and ate only the sunflower seeds one day, you would end up throwing out all the other uneaten seeds when you went to refill the feed cup. Also, with different seeds in different cups, you will find that your pet will not be throwing seeds everywhere as it searches out the kinds of seed it wants.

I prefer to purchase bulk seed by the pound in a pet shop. This way, you have a good idea that the seed is fresh. If you own one or just a few birds and buy small amounts of seed at a time and you have room in your refrigerator, you can store the packages of seed in there, so it will stay fresh longer and also will not attract bugs. A bug or two in the seed will not harm your bird; just think of it as added protein. But too many bugs could mean very old seed, which would not be good for the bird. Some boxes of bird seed may have been on the shelf for so long that the seed is old and dried out. Old, dried, dead seeds have no nutritive value for birds. If you are in doubt whether the seeds are fresh, take a handful and sprout them. If fresh, at least 90% of the seeds should sprout.

If you own quite a few birds, as we do, you can purchase your seed in 50- and 100-pound sacks. We buy a supply of seed to last for one month. Purchasing the seed in large quantities is quite a bit cheaper than buying it by the pound. The seeds are transferred from their original sacks (of burlap or paper) to large metal trash cans which are kept in a shed, where we store all our feed and supplies for our birds. Each kind of seed is put into a different trash can. The metal trash cans with tight-fitting lids keep out insects, mice, and rats, and the seed stays fresh, clean, and dry.

Fruits, Vegetables, and Soft Food   Many bird owners usually feed their pets in the traditional manner, offering an assortment of dry seeds as the staple diet. In their native habitats, *Brotogeris* parakeets do consume some mature seeds, but much of their diet consists of fruits, blossoms, and similarly soft vegetable matter. As keepers of birds in captivity, it is our responsibility to supply a varied diet for our feathered friends, since they cannot seek out the foods to which they are accustomed or which are needed to balance their diet.

There are many fruits and vegetables that can be fed to your pet. Every day, all of our birds receive apples, oranges, peas (fresh or frozen), corn (fresh or frozen), grated beets and carrots, and fresh chopped spinach. Many days I serve some additional foods for variety, such as grapes, cherries, pomegranate, romaine lettuce, plums, pears, bananas, peaches, celery leaves, squash (green or yellow), papaya, wheat bread, dry dog kibble, and monkey chow. Most Grey-cheeked Parakeets love monkey chow which has been soaked in water to a mushy consistency. The monkey-chow biscuits will absorb the water and take on a soft, spongy texture. The monkey-chow biscuit in this form is what many Grey-cheeked Parakeets are weaned on in quarantine stations when first brought here to the U.S.

I never feed avocado to any of my birds. I know of many pet birds that ate some avocado and died within a day. Some birds cannot digest this particular fruit and may die if even a small amount is eaten. I would rather be safe than sorry, so I have chosen not to feed avocado.

Some individuals will refuse to eat or even sample fruits and vegetables. You should still continue to offer a variety of produce to these birds. All of a sudden, many will start to eat other foods besides dry seed. Just be patient with these finicky birds till they find something that they like. I have found that most *Brotogeris* parakeets generally will eat a well-balanced diet of almost any fruits and vegetables which is offered to them. Never use spoiled or rotten produce, and make certain that all fruits and vegetables are washed thoroughly before being offered, to ensure that they are free from insecticide.

Sprouted Seed   I have found that a very large majority of our birds enjoy eating sprouted seed. Fresh sprouted seed is an inexpensive and nourishing food that shows a high increase in vitamin content, compared to the dry-seed stage. It is very nutritious for the birds and easily digested by their young chicks.

There are four seeds that I generally sprout for our birds, but you can add additional kinds, if you wish. Many times I alternate seeds just for variety, using barley, wheat, or pigeon mix in place of canary seed. This will help give the birds a varied diet, so they will not become bored with the same food each day. I will now describe how I prepare my sprouted seeds, but remember, you can ad-lib to your liking, as I do, giving the birds a refreshing change in their usual fare.

I use one cup each of sunflower seed and safflower seed and one-quarter cup each of white millet and canary seed. I mix all four together in a plastic bucket. I then add approximately one gallon of cold water and one teaspoon of powdered calcium propionate to the seeds and mix everything together thoroughly. The calcium propionate is a preservative; it is very important that this is included to help prevent the seeds from molding. Calcium propionate can also prevent and cure crop mold, so in very small amounts it can be beneficial for the birds. The seeds are left to soak in the bucket for eighteen to twenty-four hours. After they have soaked, they are then dumped into another bucket with many very small holes on the bottom. The holes must be smaller than the seeds so they will not go through. It is best if the entire bottom of the bucket has holes.

The way I make holes in the bottom of a plastic bucket is with a thin pointed rod (like a metal knitting needle) about twelve inches long. I heat the rod over an open flame till it is very hot, and then puncture the bottom of the bucket with the hot rod repeatedly, until it starts to cool. I continue to heat the rod and punch holes till the entire bottom is filled with holes. With this method of punching holes the edges of these openings will be melted smooth. You will find it much easier to stir the seeds when the holes are smooth. You can also use a drill to make holes on the bottom of a bucket, but you will find that with this method the holes will be somewhat rough.

After the seeds are put into the bucket with the holes, they are rinsed very well with cold water. The seeds will remain in this bucket for twenty to forty-eight hours, until they start to sprout. In the warmer weather the seeds sprout faster, and in cooler weather it takes a little longer. I stir the seeds a few times a day to prevent them from sticking together and spoiling. I have found that the lower part of the bucket is warmer, making the seeds germinate faster on the bottom. So this stirring is very important to keep the seeds loose and fresh for even sprouting. If the bucket of sprouting seed is left unstirred for over twenty-four hours, the bottom seeds could start to spoil and mold. You must discard the entire bucket of sprouted seeds at any sign of spoilage, such as a foul smell or seeds that are sticky or fuzzy in appearance. Even if only a few seeds go bad, you still must throw away the whole batch of sprouted seeds and start over.

When the seeds start to sprout, it is time to feed them to the birds. If you have a single pet or just a few birds, you can sprout about a cup of seeds at a time, using a small plastic colander instead of a large bucket. Once the seeds start to sprout, they can be stored for a day or two in the refrigerator and used as needed.

Keep in mind that sprouted seeds are fed as an additional food, not to replace the dry seed that should be kept in the cage for your bird at all times.

Water   Drinking water for your bird should be kept fresh by changing it daily. Many birds deposit fruit, vegetables, seed, and various other materials in their water cup. If this is left too long, it will foul the water, which could cause your pet to become ill. Try to place the drinking water in a location where your bird's droppings will not fall inside the cup and cause the water to become foul. This means you should not set up perches or swings directly above the feeding vessels. Each time the water is changed, the bowl or cup should be thoroughly scrubbed, washed with a detergent, and rinsed completely before being put back in the cage. If this is not done, a filmy residue will form on the inside of the water receptacle, and the growing bacteria could be harmful to your bird. If you use a tube drinker, it too must be cleaned daily. You should scrub the tube out each day with a toothbrush or a baby-bottle brush. Be sure to wash out the tube's base as well.

If more than one bird is kept in a cage, it is vitally important that the drinking water is kept absolutely clean. If the water is not clean and one of the birds in the cage becomes sick, all the birds could come down with the illness because they all drink the same water. If a bird is removed from a cage because of an illness, be sure that the cage as well as all feed cups are cleaned thoroughly, so the other birds will have a fighting chance not to contract the same illness. Be sure to keep everything just as clean as possible.

Treats   Some of the treats for birds that you will encounter on your visit to a pet shop or grocery store will be things such as spray millet; various seeds which have been formed into a bell, heart, or other shape; honey sticks, which also contain an assortment of seeds; and boxes of tidbits for your bird. You will find that different stores generally carry different kinds of bird treats, depending on the brands they stock.

Other foods can also be used as treats to offer your bird. A small dog biscuit (perhaps a kind that comes in assorted shapes and colors) will be fun for the bird to play with and eat. There are breakfast cereals birds love to nibble on, such as Zoom, Cheerios, corn flakes, and other wheat and corn cereals. Just a morsel or two should be offered per day. Stay away from sugar-coated cereals for your bird. Other possibilities are: a raw peanut in the shell; a bit of graham cracker or other kind of cracker; mynah-bird pellets; popped popcorn without butter; a piece of dry dog kibble, or a monkey-chow biscuit.

I know of many pet birds that are allowed to sample all sorts of food from the dining table. I personally do not recommend allowing a bird to eat the food we eat. Foods which are greasy, over-buttered, or sugared could harm your pet. One should use discretion when it comes to choosing treats for one's bird. Also, treats should not interfere with your pet's normal diet. If so, you should cut back on the portions of treats which are offered, or ration the treats to small amounts every other day. Remember, treats should be nourishing additions to an already good, balanced diet.

Vitamins   Vitamins especially for birds can be purchased at a pet store, in powder or liquid form. The liquid vitamins are water soluble, usually pleasant tasting, and can easily be added to your bird's drinking water. If your bird insists on bathing in its water dish, a vitamin powder may be a better choice. If you sprinkle the powder in the seed cup, most of it will just go to the bottom and not be eaten by the bird. The best place for the powder is on your bird's fruits, vegetables, or sprouted seeds. Just be sure the vitamin powder is made to be used on the food, not in the drinking water. After you cut up the washed fruits and vegetables, sprinkle the powder on them. The powder will stick to the damp food, and as the food is eaten by the bird, so are the vitamins. Be sure you serve this in a separate bowl, not mixed in with the bird's dry seeds.

I use a water-soluble vitamin powder for my birds, called Headstart. Generally used for poultry, it is strictly for mixing in the drinking water. I stir one-quarter teaspoon of Headstart into a quart of fresh water. It will immediately dissolve in the water, turning it a light yellow color. This water must be changed daily.

For my pairs of birds which are set up for breeding, I add just a little cod-liver oil and wheat-germ oil to the fruits and vegetables, coating them very lightly. I then sprinkle on a small amount of vitamin powder which is made to go on your bird's food. The cod-liver oil, which has vitamins A and D, helps to keep your bird in good health and gives the feathers sheen. Wheat-germ oil, being the richest source of vitamin E, aids the reproductive process, increasing fertile egg production and sperm.

If your bird is fed a proper diet consisting of fresh seeds and fruit and vegetables, very little vitamin supplement is required. Too much of the vitamin supplement added to your bird's food could do more harm than good.

Other Dietary Needs   There are a few other things your bird will need to round out a well-balanced diet. There should be a mineral block or a cuttlebone in the bird's cage at all times. Not only will it help to keep the beak trim and give the bird something to chew on, it will provide calcium and salt, which are essential for your bird. Your pet should also have access to health grit of some sort. This can be lightly sprinkled in the seed or on the floor of the cage, or can be offered in a small bowl. Oyster shell for birds can also be offered along with the grit. This helps to grind up food and also contains minerals needed to keep your bird in good health. There are even some all-in-one mineral blocks for birds which contain all the grit, oyster shell, and minerals needed. Such mineral blocks can be very convenient for you and your bird.

The Grey-cheek as a Pet

In the Home A bird which is kept indoors as a house pet and is rarely let out of its cage to play and exercise is usually an unhappy bird and not much fun for the person who owns the bird. Your bird should be an affectionate companion to you and your entire household. Your home should be your bird's world, where it's allowed a certain amount of freedom out of its cage to exercise and explore. When your bird is at liberty in the house, you should be around to supervise its frolicking. This is for its well-being as well as yours. A bird should never be left out of its cage when you are away from the house. Many accidents can and do happen when pet birds have the run of the house and no one is home to keep an eye on them. I have heard of several occasions where dogs and cats put an end to a pet bird, and even once about a pet snake that devoured the family bird. Even if your bird has a playground on which to play and exercise, it may not stay there the entire time it is out of the cage. Parrots are very much like children. If they think that you are not watching them, they will take off and explore. No two birds are alike in their actions and personalities. One may take off and look through the house for you, while another may decide that climbing the living-room curtains and chewing on the furniture is lots more fun. Do not trust them on the basis of the way they act when they are in front of you. They may decide to investigate the house out of curiosity when you are not around, possibly doing some damage to your furnishings or even to themselves.

Be very careful when using insecticides in the house. Ordinary insect sprays are not intended for use around birds and could be fatal to your pet: purchase only a product that can be used safely near birds. Most sprays made of pyrethrins are safe. The two I use with great success in our home and aviaries are Camicide and Hargate.

Many common house plants are poisonous to birds, such as philodendrons, ivy plants, and poinsettia. If eaten, they could prove fatal to your bird. So be careful not to let your bird climb around your house plants. Also take care not to set up your bird's cage near a house plant, as the bird may reach the plant and chew on it, or the plant could grow unnoticed into your pet's cage.

The kitchen can be a hazardous place for your bird. If you are cooking with a Teflon-coated pan and all the liquid boils dry, the pan can give off poisonous fumes. If your bird is in the kitchen at the time, it could die from inhaling the vapors from the pan. Also, a pot of boiling liquid on the stove could be a disaster for a free-roaming pet. Be sure you do not do any cooking with your bird on your shoulder.

I believe that a pet bird is usually better off with its flight feathers clipped. No matter how careful one is, the possibility of a fully flighted pet bird escaping through an open window or door is great. Yes, I do realize that most windows have screens, but I know of pets that neatly chewed a round hole in the screen and escaped. I have heard of other cases where a startled bird flew out a door just as someone was entering it. What happens is that birds instinctively fly toward the light, which means doors and windows. Also, if a fully flighted bird out of its cage is startled and takes to the air, it could fly smack into a glass window or mirror and break its wing, or even its neck. I know of pets that died days later from an injury to the head.

You should never take your bird outdoors on your shoulder unless the flight feathers are well clipped. Even with just a few long flights grown in, the bird could get some lift, if frightened, and fly into the street or over a building. I believe that the reasons for keeping your pet bird clipped outweigh the arguments for keeping it flighted. Use common sense and remember that an unclipped bird, even a tame one, may fly away if given the slightest chance.

Taming   If you are going to purchase a Grey-cheeked Parakeet, you should get one that is already tame and sweet. As I stated earlier, over ninety percent of the Grey-cheeked Parakeets imported into our country are young birds that are already extremely tame. They are very curious and will usually jump right onto a hand that is offered to them. They are ready to go to permanent homes to give and receive love.

If you decide to purchase a bird that is not tame, try to get one that is as young as possible. This will be quite difficult, as most of the young *Brotogeris* parakeets look the same as adults. Do not be fooled by a bird with light gray fuzz (this is an undercoat of soft feathers that are known as down) showing on the chest or other areas of its body, as this usually means nothing more than that the bird is probably a feather plucker. Regardless of its sex, any bird can be tamed with time and patience. Both males and females make very affectionate pets. Taming should be done one-on-one, which means that no other birds are loose in the same room.

The taming process will be much easier if the bird has its flight feathers clipped. Clipping these feathers is not at all painful or cruel. If you attempt to tame a bird which is fully flighted, you will find yourself wasting valuable training time retrieving the bird as it flies through the house. The bird could even become so

Above: This cage is suitable for a Grey-cheek or other *Brotogeris* pet. With the playground on top, once the cage door is opened, the bird can climb right up. Below: A playground designed for Cockatiels is perfect for Grey-cheeks. With food, water, and toys at hand, it will provide many hours of entertainment.

My son, Larry, showers attention and love on Peppy, his pet Grey-cheek. Peppy quickly learned to talk and was eager to learn tricks, because Larry made the frequent training sessions a fun time for the bird. Pet birds need the exercise and entertainment of excursions outside the cage.

frightened that taming may become next to impossible. When you purchase your bird, ask to have the bird's wings clipped, if this has not been done already.

There are many different styles in which the wings could be clipped. Some prefer to leave the first few outer flight feathers on each wing long, trimming the remaining primary and secondary flight feathers. I personally disagree with this, as I have seen birds still capable of some flight gaining height and flying away. Others like to clip only one wing to unbalance the bird, so it will go straight down without flying at all. I am not particularly fond of this style either, because the bird may fall from some place fairly high and injure itself. The procedure I have always followed is to cut all the primaries, but none of the secondaries, of both wings, also being very careful not to cut off more than half of the feather. This will hamper the bird's flight, but it can still catch itself if it falls. This style also looks very neat when the bird has its wings folded.

If you are not experienced at clipping a bird's wings, have a reliable bird dealer or a vet do it for you. If it is done incorrectly, the bird could end up damaged for life. I have seen many badly butchered birds. Some had the feathers cut so close to the skin that the bird could not molt naturally, and new feathers painfully grew through the short feather shafts remaining. Others had bloody wings, and some had part of their wing cut right off. I know of one person that lost her pet when an inexperienced person cut the wing, causing the bird to go into shock and die. I am not trying to scare anyone into not having their pet's wings trimmed. All I am saying is, be careful, or have someone with experience do this for you. I definitely am a firm believer in keeping a pet bird's wings clipped!

Keep in mind that the cut flight feathers will in time fall out and be replaced by new ones. The time when the bird goes through a molt will determine when the flights will need trimming again. Generally, new flight feathers will come through six to eight months after the trimming. So be sure to keep an eye on the bird, or otherwise one day your pet could fly out the door unexpectedly.

Once you get your bird home, you can start taming it immediately. The longer your bird sits untouched, the harder it will be to tame. Some people believe that a new bird should be left alone at first, for about two weeks. But all that is accomplished in that period is two weeks of time wasted.

The taming of an untamed bird should be done by a person who has self-confidence and will be dedicated to the task. Very young children should not undertake the taming lessons, but they will have much fun with an already tamed pet. Also keep in mind that there is no set time on how long it takes to tame a wild bird. It could take a short time or a very long time, depending on the individual bird as well as on how much time and effort you devote to it.

The first taming lesson should be no longer than a half hour. It is best if only one person does the taming. An untamed bird will only become confused if more than one person tries to tame it. There should be no distractions in the room during the half hour of taming; it should be done in the quietest part of your home. Take the bird out of its cage and sit down close to the floor (preferably carpeted). The bird will jump from your hands onto the floor. Keep retrieving the bird and putting it on your index finger to perch. Soon it will become tired of jumping and will remain on your finger. Let the bird sit there for awhile; try not to move, or you may startle it, and it may jump back onto the floor. Talk softly to the bird while it sits on your finger. When you feel that the bird has started to settle down, try very slowly to get the bird to climb up onto the index finger of your

Above: Provided with a bowl of fresh water, most *Brotogeris* will climb right in and enjoy themselves. Facing page: Pets and houseplants may not mix well; in this case, the loss is the geranium's. Below: Corky, our pet Cobalt-wing, enjoys supervised visits to the garden.

other hand. Gently put your finger up to the bird's lower breast and softly push. If all goes well, the bird will climb up onto the offered finger. If the bird should jump down instead, retrieve the bird and start the procedure over again. Once your bird will climb from finger to finger, as if climbing a ladder, the rest of the taming will be simple.

If the bird is a "nipper," you could put on a pair of cotton garden gloves or any pair of tight-fitting gloves. Keep in mind that most parrots are more afraid of gloves than the human hand, so this can sometimes make taming more difficult. Once the bird will sit on your finger, the gloves should be removed and not used again for the remainder of the training lesson.

As your bird is handled gently and becomes finger-tame, it will lose its fear of humans. It will soon be riding on your shoulders and climbing up and down your arms. It will beg for attention, wanting out of its cage to be with you. My son, Larry, has a pet Grey-cheeked parakeet which is so fond of him that it will run across the floor to follow him from room to room. He has given the bird lots of love, and the bird knows it and returns the love and affection. His little pet just loves to be carried around, being petted and scratched. Many birds love having the backs of their necks and heads scratched. Try this, once your bird is tame and has gained your trust. It may soon be bending its head, waiting to have it scratched.

No bird is a mean bird, but birds are distrustful and frightened of strange things. Once a bird discovers that there is nothing to be frightened of, it will settle down. You will find that pet birds have wonderful personalities, and will respond with love to the owners who take the time to understand them and care for their needs.

Talking Grey-cheeked Parakeets, and other *Broto-geris* species as well, can learn to talk. I would not consider these birds in the top-ten list of best talkers, but with persistence many do learn to speak quite a few words and phrases. Some learn not only to talk but to mimic sounds like crying, laughing, or coughing, and various whistles. Friends of ours have a pet Grey-cheeked Parakeet that lives in harmony with two Cockatiels. Not only did the Grey-cheek learn to make Cockatiel sounds, it has also picked up words from the Cockatiel that talks. Our pet Grey-cheek, called Peaches, learned to say *pretty bird* as her first words; now, when I walk into the room, the first thing she says is *pretty bird*. I had placed three other Grey-cheeked Parakeets in the same room with her, in another cage. These were older birds, at least two years of age, which were soon going to be sexed surgically and set up for breeding. Within a week, two out of the three birds were also saying *pretty bird*, which they picked up from Peaches. So, many times, if you have a pet bird in the house that is a good talker, it can teach another bird that is kept close by to speak too. Birds do learn to talk quickly from other birds. We also have a pet White-winged Parakeet that quickly learned to make kissing sounds. He is so cute, as he reaches over to give you a kiss, complete with the sound affects!

When starting out to teach your pet to talk, begin with a simple word. Most often the first words one works with are *hi* or *hello*. Work with one word or phrase at a time until the bird can say it clearly. The lesson should be no longer than ten minutes at a time, or your pet will become bored and lose interest. Try not to have any distractions during the lesson. Two or three lessons a day will be more than sufficient. When you have your pet out just for play time, you can repeat the word you have been trying to teach it, while you are playing. I have found that many birds practice talking as they chatter to themselves, usually in the morning while they are in their cages. Listen carefully as your pet chatters, and you may

Above: This "tossed salad," made up daily, consists of sprouted seed and cut-up fruits and vegetables. Below: A bucket of the sprouting mix. Sometimes, instead of calcium propionate, I use one teaspoon of liquid household bleach per gallon of water for the initial eighteen-hour soaking.

A Grey-cheeked Parakeet preparing to dig into its dish of nutritious goodies. This is the amount offered daily to a pair, but even a singly kept pet should be allowed this kind of variety. A pair feeding young is given twice this amount, or more.

hear among the gibberish its first attempts to say the word you have been working on. The word may not be clear in the beginning, but with work and practice it will improve.

Many bird owners use speech-training records or tapes to teach their bird to talk. These records and tapes can be purchased at a pet shop. Some pet owners have taped their own voices, repeating the lesson over and over and playing it a few times a day for ten minutes at a time. Records and tapes do work, but I still feel that in working with your pet bird one-on-one you will have more success and usually quicker results.

There is no need to cover your bird's cage or darken the room during a speech lesson. And please resist sounding like a parrot when you are teaching your bird to talk. The more human your voice sounds, the better your bird's speech will be. Remember to speak slowly and clearly, and try to use the same tone of voice during each lesson. Most birds will begin to talk more quickly if you speak at a higher pitch. Many birds pick up words and sounds from children because their voices are naturally high-pitched. Keep in mind that all birds are individuals. Some will make excellent talkers, repeating words and phrases and even learning to whistle songs.

Others remain poor talkers, learning to speak only a word or two. Many times it is the trainer's fault that a bird doesn't talk more. After a couple of words are learned, the lessons cease, and so does the talking. The more time you spend on the lessons, the wider your pet's vocabulary can be. Just be patient, and work with your bird daily to improve its vocabulary. Remember that the extent of your bird's talking depends greatly on the amount of time spent.

Tricks   Once you and your pet have developed a close, trusting relationship, you can attempt to teach it some tricks. This will require much time and plenty of patience. Pushing a small cart, picking up and placing objects into a container, walking a tightrope, ringing a bell, riding on a small car, playing dead in your hand, and rolling over are some possibilities, and the list can go on and on. Watch your bird when it is playing. Maybe you will see something your pet does naturally that you can work with and get it to perform on demand. Perhaps you can get your bird to roll a small ball or marble placed in front of it. Use your imagination to think up various tricks you may want to teach your pet. Just as in teaching your bird to talk, do not overdo the training sessions. Work on a trick no more than fifteen minutes at a time, or your student will more than likely become bored with the whole thing.

If you want to teach your pet to climb a rope, use a heavy cord. This way, the bird can easily hold on with its feet. Thin string, such as kite string, just will not do.

Teaching your bird to open a small box is another cute trick. Put some treats it is especially fond of inside a box that can be opened easily. Let it take some food from the inside, then close the box. If it cannot figure out how to open it, you can help out a few times. Soon it will learn how to open the box and get the goodies out. You can use an oblong drawer-type matchbox that is taped to a table or glued to a small board. Show your pet what is inside and then close the box, leaving it open just a crack. Soon your bird will learn to pull open the drawer and retrieve the prize inside.

You can give your pet a cardboard tube just large enough for it to crawl through. As soon as the bird enters the tube, cover one end with your hand so that the bird must go through the tube and out the other end. With a little work your bird will soon be walking through a tunnel when given the tube.

Your pet will also ride on a toy car. Equip the car with a perch so the bird can sit on it comfortably. Attach a

Above: A hand-reared Grey-cheeked chick, just weaned. The tameness that comes from hand-rearing is the best foundation for teaching a bird tricks. Below: Larry taught Peppy to lie calmly on her back, a most unnatural position for a bird.

Above: Debbie, my daughter, reaches down to give Corky, our pet Cobalt-wing, a kiss. Corky, loving all this attention, is always making kissing noises in order to get a kiss. Below: This Grey-cheek, like most tame parrots, enjoys having its neck and cheeks scratched.

long string to the car and gently pull the car around the room. If the bird flies or jumps off, just put it back. Once your pet enjoys this ride, you can then get it to ride on an electric automobile. Just think how cute it would be to play on the kitchen linoleum with your bird on a slow-moving electric car. If a friend comes over, the two of you could sit on the floor, passing the car to one another, with your bird as a passenger.

In a few short lessons my son, Larry, taught his Grey-cheeked Parakeet to stay and come on command. As he sat on the floor, he would put his bird just a few feet in front of him and say, "Stay!" If the bird would start to run toward him, he would put the bird back in the same spot and cover it with his hand for a moment and repeat, "Stay!" Once the bird would stay in the same spot for a few moments, he would then pat the floor and say, "Come!" When his bird came to him, it was praised and petted and picked up, as this bird just loves attention and cuddling. Within a few lessons his bird was better trained than my Doberman Pinscher! Larry also taught his Grey-cheeked Parakeet to play dead in his hand. He would stroke and play with the bird. This parakeet just loves to be tickled under the wing, so while scratching and play-ing with the bird, Larry would gently turn it on its back. He would continue to scratch the Grey-cheeked Parakeet under the wing while it lay on its back. Soon the bird had no fear of lying on its back, and it will lie relaxed in that position, sometimes playing with its toes. It is most im-portant never to drop a bird when it is in this position, for it could become scared to the point of never trusting you or allowing it to be held this way again.

There are very many tricks that can be taught to your bird. Be creative and try to invent special tricks that suit your pet's temperament. Just remember a few simple points. It is best if only one person conducts the training lesson, with no distractions in the same room. Also, if another person attempts to teach the bird the trick before it has it down pat, this may only fluster the bird and make it more difficult to learn. Work on one trick at a time, and do not start to teach another trick before your bird knows the first one, otherwise all you will be doing is confusing and discouraging your pet. Be very patient with your bird. Even if the trick you are teaching is an easy one, it may take your pet a while to learn it. Keep in mind that you have to communicate with your bird, so it will know exactly what you expect. Once your pet knows what it is you are trying to get it to do, the rest is easy. In teaching a pet anything, the main thing is for the owner or teacher to have lots of patience!

Traveling with Your Pet   If your bird is tame, has clipped flight feathers, and is not nervous when taken out of its cage, you can take your pet on outdoor trips with you. Trips to the park or beach are fine, as long as you do not keep your pet in direct sunlight for long periods at a time. This could be very harmful to your bird. Also be sure to keep an eye out for loose dogs that might harm your pet.

Traveling in a car is fine, as long as it is not too hot in the car. Birds have become dehydrated quickly and can have a heat stroke. If your bird is tame and likes sitting on your shoulder or on the car seat, be sure all the windows are rolled up so your pet will not fall out.

I recommend having a small carrying cage on hand at all times, even on short trips. This comes in handy if you must leave your bird in the car for just a minute, or if your pet becomes nervous and jumpy. Your pet may even feel more secure in a carrying cage while traveling. A carrying cage is a wooden box with openings in the top or sides covered with wire mesh. The mesh provides ventilation for your pet, but it also allows you to observe your pet while traveling. Also, most birds prefer to be

Above: For the feather trim I prefer, about eight of the outer primaries are cut even with the primary coverts. Below: This shows what the trimmed wing looks like. The next step is to trim the other wing the same way.

Peppy is letting Corky know that she got to my shoulder first and to back off. *Brotogeris* can be quite protective of their owners and aggressive toward other people as well as other birds.

able to see out while traveling, especially tame pets. Carrying cages can be purchased in most pet shops and are quite inexpensive, or they can easily be made at home. If you own a few birds, you can also make or purchase a carrying cage with a divider to make it two cages in one. This allows two birds to be transported in compartments, so no fighting can occur. There should be only one door for each compartment, which must close securely so there will be no chance of escape. A handle should be on top of the cage for convenience. You will find these cages very handy for traveling to the vet or even to a friend's house.

If you are going a short distance, it will not be necessary to put a cup of water into the carrying cage. Usually the water just spills, and the bird ends up wet. You can bring along a jug of fresh water and a cup in case you have car trouble, or if the trip turns out to be longer than expected. If you are going to someone's home, you should offer the bird water in a cup as soon as you arrive. Seed, moist bread, and apple should be available in the carrying cage for most trips.

The cage can be placed on the seat or the floor in the car, but make sure it is not in direct sunlight. Also, never leave a bird in a hot car with the windows rolled up. I know some people who were traveling in the hot summer months and left their birds in the car for about thirty minutes with the windows just partly opened. When they returned to their car, the birds had all died. So be very careful when traveling in very hot weather, as well as in extremely cold weather. If the weather is very hot, a damp towel covering most of the cage will help to keep the bird cool. If your bird is nervous when traveling, it is best to keep the carrying cage covered with a towel anyway, as this will help to keep the bird as calm and quiet as possible. If the bird becomes excited and starts jumping around in the cage, it could end up injuring itself. Try not to startle the bird by bumping the carrying cage or driving fast over a bumpy road.

Some people take their pet birds on vacation with them. I know a family that installed a small parrot stand in the window of their motor home. Their bird just loves to travel and go camping with the family, as it sits on the stand watching the cars and scenery through the closed glass window. At the campground it waits patiently on the picnic table for a toasted hamburger bun. That bird is part of the family.

When Fred and I go on vacation trips, we either take our camper or stay in a hotel. We have traveled with as many as thirty-five parrot chicks of all kinds which had to be hand-fed. The chicks have to be over a week old if we are to travel in the camper. I put about seven chicks together in a small cardboard box with a layer of pine shavings, and cover the box with heavy bath towels to keep the heat in. Of course, I have some holes on the side of the box for air. If the chicks are younger, we will get a hotel room so the chicks can be on a heating pad. I take along an ice chest for the hand-rearing formula and a hot plate for warming it. So, you see, it is not impossible to travel with birds of any age.

Leaving Your Bird at Home   If you plan to go away on vacation and leave your bird behind, be sure that your pet will be adequately taken care of. You can leave your bird with a relative, a neighbor, or a friend. Be sure to leave the "bird-sitter" plenty of food and also written instructions for the care of your bird. Be sure to check where your bird-sitter is planning to set up your bird's cage, making sure it will be out of drafts and direct sunlight. Be sure to write down the telephone numbers of the place you will be staying and your bird's vet. This way, if a problem should arise, the person who has been left in charge of your pet can call for information or get help if

Above: A pair of Grey-cheeks guarding their Budgie-sized nest box. Facing page: Our first pairs of Cobalt-wings; both pairs went to nest in the same box. Below: Grey-cheeks do not chew much, but many do like to alter the nest-box entrance.

needed. Try to leave your pet with someone who knows the bird and is knowledgeable about birds and their care. If possible, call the bird-sitter periodically to be sure that everything is fine and to see if there are any questions.

If you want to leave your bird at home, you can give your house key to a friend or a neighbor so he can tend the bird while you are gone. Leaving the bird at home may be less stressful for it than being moved to unfamiliar surroundings. Try to find a person who will feed and check up on your pet both morning and evening, to make sure everything is fine. This double-checking is just in case of an accident, such as the bird injuring itself on the cage or suddenly becoming ill. It never hurts to be safe.

If you plan to go away for just one night and you cannot find someone to take care of your pet, you can leave it home alone if there is plenty of food and water in the cage. You should leave a light on. This way, if your pet is spooked during the night (by an earthquake, storm, or the telephone ringing), it will not hurt itself on the cage as it might in the dark.

Keep in mind that many vets and pet shops will board birds for a small fee. So if you cannot find someone to bird-sit, ask your vet, or call around to find a reliable pet shop.

Breeding

In the Wild   In their native environment, *Brotogeris* parakeets usually are seen in flocks, many times numbering a hundred or more. As they fly or perch in trees, they are extremely noisy, screeching and chattering. These birds thrive on companionship much of the year, but when they go to nest, they pair off and nest separately, one pair per nesting cavity. Some species will nest in hollow tree limbs or trunks which have been worked already by other birds or animals. The hen will lay her eggs on the decaying wood or moist moss. She will incubate the eggs, while the male stays nearby during the day, guarding the nest. Some of the *Brotogeris* species will nest in termite mounds found in trees. The termites make a nest in the shape of a big ball about two and a half feet in diameter, usually about five or six feet from the ground. The pair will tunnel their way into the termite nest, excavating an area inside just large enough for them to raise their young. In most cases there will only be one pair of nesting birds per termite mound. This is not an abandoned termite nest, so if an intruder should scratch the surface of the mound, hundreds of termites would rush out to protect their home. Why the birds are allowed by the termites to nest inside their mound is unknown, but the termites never bother the parents or chicks. As soon as the young birds leave the nest, the termites seal up the hole and tunnel, so it appears that the mound was never disturbed.

It would be next to impossible to duplicate exactly the natural situations in which these parakeets nest. All we

My feeding program emphasizes fresh fruits and vegetables. A nutritious and varied diet is extremely important when it comes to setting up *Brotogeris* parakeets for breeding.

Above: As I was placing a dish of soft food in the cage, one of this Grey-cheeked pair flew right out the door and attacked my hand. When breeding, they can become quite vicious. Below: Note the characteristic *Brotogeris* beak shape of this Cobalt-wing, adapted to a diet of soft foods.

can do for our birds in captivity is to try various nesting arrangements until we find the one that is right for a particular pair of birds, that will induce them to go to nest and produce young. Keep in mind that all birds react differently and are individuals, and that what may work well for one pair of birds may not be suitable for another.

Setting Up for Breeding   There are various ways to house *Brotogeris* parakeets if you intend to breed them. They can be set up for breeding in small cages or in large aviaries, indoors or outdoors. This just depends on personal preference, apart from the space available and weather conditions. Here where we live in southern California, all our birds can remain outdoors throughout the year. In Illinois, our friend Tony Silva must breed all his birds indoors, as the birds would not be able to take the severe winter weather.

Many types of cages and aviaries can be purchased, or you can construct your own. It is not difficult to build an aviary or cage; almost any handy person can do it. Cages can be constructed out of wood and wire mesh, or entirely of mesh. With the special pliers and clips on the market, anyone can quickly clip together a cage of wire mesh on all six sides, and then cut an opening to make a door on the front.

We have large outdoor aviaries with cages set up inside for breeding small parrots like *Brotogeris*. It is very easy to keep your birds healthy and clean by having a mesh floor. This way, all the extra fruit and vegetable matter falls through the mesh and will not become rancid while still within the birds' reach. Their droppings also go through the bottom, which keeps the birds clean. Our cages for breeding these birds range from twenty-four-inch cubicles up to flights three feet wide by six feet deep by six feet high. Most are made of ½ x ¼-inch mesh. We have found this size to be very successful in keeping mice from gaining entry, disturbing the birds, and eating the seed. Mice can upset the birds when they are nesting, and possibly spread disease as well. All our cages are set up inside aviaries or large safety cages, so if a bird escapes from a cage it will not get away. A safety door is crucial. With just one escape prevented, that little extra precaution will have paid for itself.

A bird that has been kept indoors must be acclimated to the outdoor weather if it is going to be set up for breeding outside. If the weather is cool in the evening, the bird must be eased outside slowly. Once the temperature is about 55°F. or more, the bird can be put outdoors for the day but must be taken indoors for the night. This should be done over a period of one month, leaving the bird out later each evening until it is left outside for the entire night. An indoor bird can be left outdoors permanently when the weather is warm and the temperature does not drop below 55°F. during the night. I have found that *Brotogeris* parakeets are fairly easy to acclimate to the outdoor weather in southern California. Once acclimated, our birds can take the winter weather very well, which can get as cold as 28°F. There are no heaters in any of our aviaries; all our birds are acclimated to our climate. When acclimating new birds, be sure that you keep a very close watch on them. You must take the birds back indoors at the first sign of possible illness (looking puffy or not bright-eyed). If you purchase birds from someone who has kept them outdoors in weather similar to yours, they can be put directly in an aviary or cage outdoors. These birds will already be acclimated to outdoor weather. Remember to house newly purchased birds separately, away from your other birds.

You can also breed birds in your house or your garage. Just be sure that during the warm summer months it does not get too hot where they are housed. Our birds can take the outdoor summer heat of 110°F., but a poorly

Above: My husband, Fred, builds many of the nest boxes we use. Below: If the box is hung inside the enclosure, inspection is easier if the lid is hinged at the back. For boxes designed to hang outside, the lid is hinged at the front.

Above: These boxes have just been lined with pieces of cork paneling, using white school glue. As the glue dries, it becomes clear. Below: A Grey-cheek with two chicks and an unhatched egg. The cork lining of this nest box has been chewed to bits.

ventilated garage or attic can become very hot and stuffy. A fan or a cooler can be helpful, but do not let it blow directly on the birds, or they may become ill.

I personally prefer to set up each pair of birds in their own cage. This way, there is no quarreling over food or nest boxes. But we have also bred these parakeets with two pairs housed together in a larger cage. They seem to do well either way; when a pair of Grey-cheeked Parakeets are ready to go to nest, they will generally nest in either situation. I have found that the these birds must be between two and three years of age to breed successfully. So don't get discouraged if your birds have not gone to nest, as many of these birds take years to settle down and mature. Remember, Grey-cheeked Parakeets are brought into U.S. quarantine stations as very young birds and will need time to mature.

Brotogeris parakeets are not sexually dimorphic. So if you want to breed these birds, it is best that they are laparoscoped to determine maturity and health status before setting up pairs.

Be sure the pairs are on a well-balanced diet of good, fresh seed and plenty of fruits and vegetables. It is very important to keep your birds in top condition, especially for breeding success. Perches must not be loose, or incomplete mating could occur and result in infertile eggs. If the birds are set up outdoors, try to give them as much privacy as possible. A pair of tame Grey-cheeked Parakeets kept in the house can also be supplied with a nest box. This way, if they should decide to go to nest, the box is already in place and they can set up housekeeping whenever they feel like doing so. I have heard stories of pairs going to nest and rearing their young right in the living room. As tame birds with no fear of humans, they will tend their eggs and chicks and just ignore the familiar sounds of the people in the household.

Keep in mind that when you are preparing to raise

birds, it is very important to keep written records, as one often tends to forget mental notes. Some things that should be jotted down are: what date each egg was laid; hatching date of each chick; the total number of eggs laid; how many were fertile and hatched; how well the parents took care of their chicks; when babies fledged and became independent—as well as many other points of possible future interest. Even such things as injuries or illnesses, with the treatments and medicines that were used, can be kept in your notes. They can be written in a notebook or even on a calendar. Thanks to the records on our birds, I can quickly look back anytime and find the information I need to know.

Nest Boxes   Though nesting in termite mounds and the hollows of trees occurs in the wild, I have found that in captivity a large majority of these birds will take quite readily to simply constructed wooden nest boxes. Some birds will use small boxes such as the Budgie-size nest box, while others prefer a larger box like those generally used for Cockatiels. Most of my *Brotogeris* pairs sleep inside the nest box at night, rather than roosting on a perch, so nest boxes are provided throughout the year for all of these species.

Wooden nest boxes can be purchased at most pet stores. Or, if you have a little extra time and a few tools (saw, hammer, drill, and nails) a nest box can easily be constructed out of quarter-inch plywood. The dimensions of the box will usually depend on the amount of space available, as well as on the preferences of the pair. The average Budgie nest box measures 8 x 8 x 6½ inches wide. The dimensions for most Cockatiel nest boxes are 10 x 10 x 11 inches deep. If for example, you have been using a Budgie box and the pair does not accept the box after a reasonable length of time (about four months), try offering a Cockatiel nest box. I have found that all birds

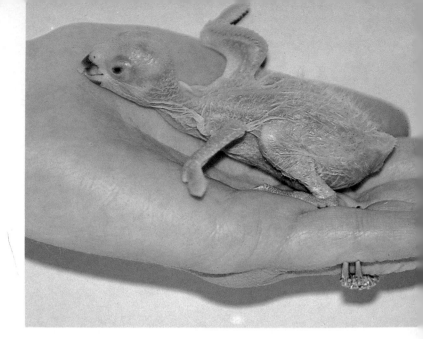

Above: At 14 days of age, this Grey-cheeked chick weighed 23.5 grams. The beak, which was light at hatching, is by now partly dark. Below: A 25-day-old Grey-cheek. The tips of the largest feathers have emerged from the sheaths.

Above: By six and a half weeks, all the tracts show feather growth. Below: Nine weeks old and eating on its own, this young Grey-cheek very much resembles an adult so far as feather color is concerned.

are individuals and have their likes and dislikes. Some pairs prefer larger boxes, while others want the smaller ones. I have even heard of Grey-cheeked Parakeets nesting in finch nest boxes, which are considerably smaller than the other kinds. Remember, what may work for one pair may not necessarily do for another.

The entrance hole of the nest box should be 2 to 2½ inches in diameter. Some birds may enlarge the entrance hole slightly. I have found that most pairs usually do not chew up their nest boxes. *Brotogeris* parakeets are not notorious chewers, like many other parrots. Conures, amazons, and macaws can destroy an entire wooden nest box in less than a week. There should be a perch or platform about two inches below the entrance hole so the pair can easily get in or out of the nest box.

The nesting materials I use in our nest boxes are pine shavings and peat moss. When setting up the nest box I put in a thin layer of damp peat moss, followed with about three inches of dry pine shavings. Do not worry about putting too much nesting material inside the box, as the pair will remove what they do not want. I have also glued pieces of cork wall paneling to the inside of the nest box, using nontoxic white school glue. This has proved to be quite successful, as the birds chew on the cork to line and build up their nest, just before the eggs are laid. The layer of cork may resemble the inside of an old tree or termite mound.

The nest box should be thoroughly cleaned once the chicks have left the nest, whether they fledge on their own or are pulled for hand-rearing. The box should be sprayed inside and out with a good mite spray and then aired out in the sun for a day or two, before being put back in with the birds. The mite spray must be made especially for use around birds. Many brands of bird spray can be purchased in pet shops. Some of the ones we have used are Cage and Aviary, Hargate, and

Camicide. All contain pyrethrins, which are not harmful to birds when used carefully.

If you are going to aviary-breed these birds, with one pair per flight, try putting in two nest boxes, one Budgie box and one Cockatiel nest box. This way, the pair can choose the size they prefer. If there will be more than one pair of birds to a flight, offer two nest boxes per pair, so the abundance of nest boxes will prevent quarreling. Once I had two pairs of Grey-cheeked Parakeets set up together with a variety of nest boxes at their disposal. Both pairs insisted on sleeping together in a small wooden finch nest box. As evening came, they would all climb into that tiny nest box, not to be heard or seen till the following day.

Cage breeding has proved to be very suitable for breeding *Brotogeris*. Nest boxes can be placed inside the cage or hung on the outside. This will depend on the type and size of the cage which is being used for breeding. Most of our cages have the nest box attached outside the cage. A hole large enough for the birds to go through is cut in the side wall of the cage where the nest-box entrance hole is. All our outdoor aviaries have a roof so they are sheltered from the rain and hot sun. In the winter the wire walls of the aviaries are covered with clear plastic sheeting to protect the birds from wind and blowing rain, which could get the cages, feed, and nest boxes wet. If the nest box gets damp while there are eggs or chicks inside, they could become chilled and die.

If a mature pair of birds do not go to nest in a reasonable amount of time (about one year), you can try different things to stimulate them. Installing pieces of cork paneling in the nest box is one possibility. A pair of our Cobalt-winged Parakeets seemed to really enjoy chewing up the cork. I have heard of a few occasions on which a large rotted log was provided for a pair of Grey-cheeked Parakeets. The birds would chew and tunnel in-

After the cork paneling is in place and the glue dry, I pour in some pine shavings, and the nest box is ready for use.

Above: For hygienic reasons, each breeding cage has its own tray. Below: Usually, breeding pairs are housed in their own cages and offered a choice of nest boxes, if space allows.

to the log and lay their eggs in the center. I have found that most of these parakeets like to construct some kind of nest inside their box, though not quite as elaborate as what a lovebird would build. My pairs of Canary-winged, Grey-cheeked, and Cobalt-winged parakeets will take all kinds of material inside their nest box, such as leaves, apple skins, orange peels, newspapers, feathers, sticks, and anything else they may find. Some people offer branches with leaves still attached, so the birds can remove what they want (bark and leaves) to line their nest box (be sure the branches have not been sprayed with insecticide and that the plant is not toxic to birds). Straw and palm fronds can also be offered, but most of my pairs have not been too excited about these as nest liners. Some breeders have even gone to the extent of building fancy nest boxes which were covered with bark or straw around the outside walls, and some have had breeding success with these specially designed nest boxes. Other bird breeders do nothing out of the ordinary: all that is supplied is a standard wooden nest box, and the pairs produce many chicks each year. It is important, therefore, to work with your birds and find out what they are happy with, so they will settle down and raise a family.

Courtship and Egg Laying   Before a *Brotogeris* pair settle down to raise a family, they will develop a pair bond. This bonding will usually be demonstrated by the pair preening and feeding each other. In most cases it is the male that feeds the hen, but if two birds are housed together and are the same sex, mutual preening and feeding can still occur. This is why surgical sexing is the best way to know if two birds set up for breeding are indeed a pair.

These birds can be observed copulating many times during the day, out on the perch. Copulation is done in the same manner as with the larger parrots. The hen lowers the front part of her body as she lifts up her tail. The male places one foot on her back, while the other foot firmly grips the perch. Then he presses his vent against hers. Copulation can last from one to five minutes. I have observed our birds copulating on many occasions, and I have found this act does not always mean that eggs are soon to follow.

When a pair is getting ready to go to nest, they will both spend a lot of time in the nest box. The material inside the nest box is dug up and kicked around, sometimes more so by the hen. Soon a concave impression is made in the nesting material, usually in the corner of the nest box.

As the time approaches for the hen to lay an egg, her lower abdomen will swell and appear to have a lump (the developing eggs). Once the swelling is present, the first egg should be laid within a week. The remaining eggs are generally laid every other day. All this time the hen will spend most of the day in the nest box, making the preparations for the clutch. Average clutch size for Grey-cheeked Parakeets is four eggs, but clutches can range from two to six eggs. Canary-winged and Cobalt-winged parakeets usually have larger clutches of five or six eggs. There is no set number of eggs a bird will lay per clutch. Every hen is an individual, so her usual clutch size may be larger or smaller than the average. Also, the number of eggs she lays may vary from clutch to clutch. The average size of the *Brotogeris* egg measures 28/32 x 23/32 inches, which is larger than a Budgie egg and a little smaller than a Cockatiel egg, but about the same size as a Peach-faced Lovebird egg.

Incubation and Hatching   The incubation period for the *Brotogeris* eggs is usually twenty-five to twenty-six days. Almost always the hen is the one that does the actual incubating. In most pairs the male stands guard

Above: The wall calendar helps me to keep track of breeding activities. It is always wise to keep records for future reference. Below: The bright light bulb of the Prob-Light makes it possible to candle an egg in a brightly lit room.

Above: Many incubators have a fan to circulate the air and adjustments to control both temperature and humidity. Below: This incubator has an automatic turner, but I still prefer to turn the eggs by hand: a half turn three to six times a day.

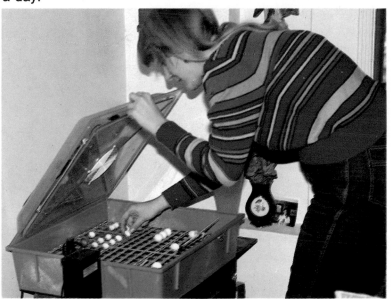

just outside the nest, entering only to feed the hen and to sleep at night. In other pairs the male may spend most of the day in the nest box keeping the hen company or helping with some of the incubation. I have found that each pair will act differently, being individuals.

Some hens start to incubate right away, with the first egg. Other hens may wait till at least three eggs are laid, and some do not start incubation till the entire clutch has been laid. Many times the hen will pluck some of her breast feathers to line the nest. I had a pair of Canary-winged Parakeets which lined the whole nest with their small, soft, green feathers. The miraculous thing was that the pair still looked smooth and in good feather.

As the time for the chicks to hatch comes closer, they will start to pip the shell. You may notice a very slight outward crack on the egg after about twenty-four or twenty-five days of incubation. Once this crack is seen, the chick could release itself from the egg within forty-eight hours. When the chicks hatch, they are sparsely covered with white down. The hen will brood and feed her chicks with help from her mate. *Brotogeris* chicks grow rapidly. At twelve days the eyes are open. By fourteen days dark feathers can be seen developing under the skin on the back and sides of the chick, which weighs in at about twenty-five grams. Very little secondary down grows in; instead, the feathers grow in rapidly, and by twenty-six days the feathers start to "pop" through the sheaths, first on the tail and wings, then on the rest of the body. Chicks will sometimes leave the nest as young as five weeks old, but the average fledging age appears to be six weeks.

Both parents will continue to feed the chicks after they have left the nest box. Usually by the time the chicks are nine weeks old, they are eating on their own. Once the young birds are independent, they should be removed from their parent's cage. If the young are left in with their parents, they may disturb the breeding pair when they return to nest, resulting in eggs being broken or dead chicks.

Nest Inspection   Inspecting the nest box to check on the well-being of your birds is, in my opinion, very important, provided your birds are accustomed to this procedure. Try to establish this as a daily routine. Once the pair go to nest, they will be used to your examining their nest box, so you can check their nest regularly without causing problems. You can be sure that the hen, eggs, and chicks are doing all right.

Most of the time the birds will be just fine with their clutch. But sometimes problems will arise, and if caught quickly, in many cases they can be corrected. A hen may become egg bound, which means she is unable to pass her egg. Spotting this in time can mean saving her life, for if she is left in this condition, she could die. A hen that is egg bound will normally have a swelling in her vent area, which is the egg that cannot be passed. The hen appears sick, with her feathers puffed, and usually is unable to fly. As she strains, she will become extremely weak, and she keeps her eyes partially shut. At this stage the hen may come out of the nest box, or she may stay inside. If she does not pass her egg, she will become exhausted and soon die. This can happen with any egg in a clutch, and it can happen with any clutch. This is why inspecting the nest box is very important. If you find a hen in this condition, she should be rushed to a vet to have the egg removed. If this is not possible, there are various measures that can be tried. A common treatment for egg binding is inserting a drop or two of warm mineral oil or olive oil into her vent. If the eyedropper is inserted too far, the egg could be broken, causing the hen's death. After the oil treatment, hold the hen for a few minutes over the steam from a tea kettle or a pot of

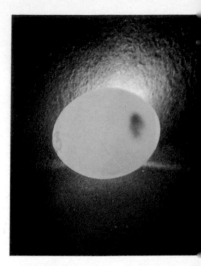

Eggs candled over a flashlight in a dark room. Above, left:
This "clear" egg could be a freshly laid, fertile egg that has
not begun to develop; on the other hand, if it has been
incubated for several days, it is infertile. Above, right: This
egg started to develop, but the embryo died for one reason
or another. Possibly the egg became chilled, or the embryo
was just weak. Below, left: A strong, well-developed embryo,
about a week old, surrounded by blood vessels. Below, right:
The fully developed chick should soon start to hatch
through the air space at the top of the egg.

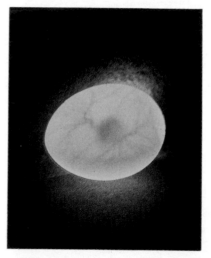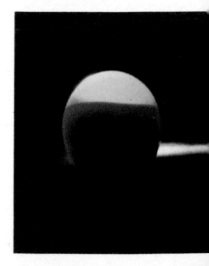

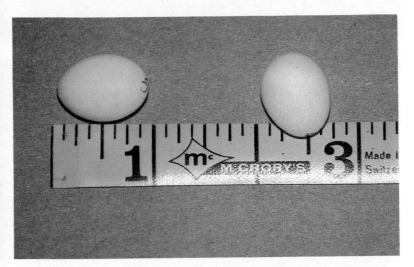

Above: Grey-cheeked Parakeet eggs. Below: Frank Lanier successfully relieved this badly egg-bound Grey-cheek using the steam method. The hen and egg were returned to the nest box, where the egg hatched twenty-six days later.

boiling water, about eight inches away. Place her in a box or small cage with no perches and put a heating pad underneath, set on Low to Medium. She should pass the egg within a few hours. Once the egg has been laid, she can be returned to her mate and nest box, with her egg. Such a hen should be watched very carefully; inspect the nest box twice daily to be sure this does not happen again. If so, the whole procedure must be repeated. Try adding more calcium and slightly more oily foods to her diet if she appears to have problems laying her eggs. There are times when the egg is hard to pass because it is soft-shelled. If you cannot get the hen to expel the egg, consult your veterinarian or an experienced bird breeder.

During your daily nest-box inspections, you could come across a slightly cracked egg. If it has been discovered in time, you may be able to repair it. If it is a hairline crack, you can seal it with a coat or two of clear nail polish, painting over the cracked area only. Once the nail polish has dried completely (in about five minutes), the egg can be returned to the nest box. If the egg is put back in the box before the polish is dry, the egg may get nesting material stuck to it, or it may stick to the hen and get broken.

While inspecting the nest boxes you may come across a hen who has stopped incubating or started to break her eggs. If so, the eggs must be removed immediately and placed in an incubator. If you should be fortunate enough to have another *Brotogeris* pair on eggs at about the same stage of incubation, the fertile eggs could be placed under that hen, along with her own, provided this does not make too many eggs for her to tend to. Eight eggs should be the very most a *Brotogeris* hen should attempt to incubate. If there are any infertile eggs, be sure to take those out, so the nest box will not be overcrowded. This way, she can concentrate on live, fertile eggs. Sometimes other species will incubate the eggs and even rear the chicks. I have found that many times Budgies and Bourke's Parakeets can be excellent foster parents. I have had the Bourke's Parakeets raise chicks of many species for me, including Cobalt-winged Parakeets.

Once the shell is pipped, the chick can take up to forty-eight hours to free itself. If a chick gets stuck in the shell, you can help it out, but this very rarely happens if parents are incubating the eggs. If the pair has been provided with water for bathing, the shell and membrane of the egg usually will not be too hard or too dry for the chick to break through.

When the chicks have hatched, you should keep a close watch on the hatchlings, inspecting the nest in the morning and again just before dark. This is to be sure the parents are brooding and feeding the chicks. If the chicks are cold or unfed, they must be removed for hand-rearing. I have heard of some pairs that pluck their chicks' down and feathers, sometimes even going to the extent of killing them. At the first sign of any trouble, such as blood on the chicks, they should be removed immediately, to be hand-fed. If the chicks are left in the nest box, the parents may eventually kill them.

If the hen is inside when you check the nest box, try not to chase her out. Inspection should only take a few seconds. If you stick your hand inside the nest box, you will more than likely get severely bitten by the bold little parent. I myself have opened a Grey-cheeked Parakeet's nest box to be surprised by the pair threatening to attack. Believe me, they will carry out their threat. Most of the other *Brotogeris* pairs will just sit still or slowly leave the box while I am inspecting it. As soon as the lid is closed, the parents will return to their box. Tame birds tend to be more bold when it comes to defending their territory. Having no fear of humans, they will fight you off, with all their power. There is no need to move the hen or to touch the eggs or chicks during your routine inspection, unless you

Above: A brood of Canary-winged Parakeets *(B. v. chiriri)*, two weeks old. Below: At three weeks old, the yellow wing coverts can be seen through the sheaths, and the beak has darkened.

Above: Five weeks old, this Canary-wing has been banded with a standard Cockatiel closed band, which bears the year, breeder's initials, and a number. Below: At five weeks, the feathers on the wings are well developed, but the body is still mostly covered with down.

suspect a problem. Should you come across a broken egg or dead chick in the nest box, these should be removed.

If the pair has been properly fed and supplied with the proper necessities for raising a family, usually very few problems arise.

Candling Eggs   Newly laid eggs are white with a pinkish cast. If an egg is fertile and developing properly, the shell will look solid white, because the egg is no longer translucent. If you compare an infertile egg to a fertile egg that has been incubated for at least a week, it is fairly easy to see the difference in color between these two eggs. An egg that has a hairline crack can dry up on the inside and appears to be a solid white color at first; as the egg ages, it turns a grayish white.

If you want to see whether the eggs are fertile and are developing properly, you can candle the eggs. You should wait at least five days after the last egg was laid by the hen. This way, you can be reasonably certain that the eggs have been incubated by the hen for at least five days, so fertility will be evident. Egg candlers can be purchased from some pet shops or through bird or poultry dealers. I use a Prob-Light put out by Medical Diagnostic Services, Inc., to candle all our eggs, from small finch eggs all the way up to macaw eggs. With the Prob-Light I can candle the eggs right in the nest box, without touching or removing the eggs. This battery-operated candler has a long handle with a very tiny, bright light bulb at the tip. When this bright bulb is placed against the shell, any developing embryo can be seen. If the egg is fertile, and has been incubated for only about five days, you will see a web of red blood vessels. In an egg that has been incubated for a longer period, a moving embryo will be visible. As the chick gets closer to hatching, the egg will appear more completely filled. It will be dark and fairly hard to see through. At this stage you will be able to see the air pocket on the large end of the egg, where the chick will pip and emerge. You can also see if the air pocket is in the wrong position (on the bottom or the side). If so, you should be prepared to assist the chick to hatch, if necessary. Many times the chick cannot hatch if it is in the wrong position inside the egg.

To make your own egg candler, get a bright flashlight and some aluminum foil. Use a pencil to make a hole in the foil, about the same diameter as the pencil. Cover the entire lens with the aluminum foil. The foil can be secured with some tape around the circumference of the flashlight. Turn on the flashlight and carefully hold the egg over the hole in the foil. As with the Prob-Light, if the egg is fertile, you will see red blood vessels. If it is getting close to the hatching stage, it will not be translucent, but you will be able to see the air space. Candling should be done in semidarkness. Be sure not to get the egg hot with the homemade candler, or it could kill the embryo.

The more eggs you inspect, the more experienced you will become. You will be able to distinguish fertile from infertile eggs after a week of incubation with just a quick glance when they are still in the nest box, even without candling. If an egg is fertile but has not hatched, you can candle the egg to see if the embryo is still alive and moving. Having a candler on hand can be very convenient when breeding birds. No matter how good you become at distinguishing fertile and infertile eggs, always candle the egg very carefully before discarding what you think may be a "bad" egg. Keep this in mind: in candling many eggs over the years, I have found some healthy, live embryos that showed no movement a couple of days before hatching, but looked dead. So if you are in doubt, leave the eggs in the incubator or under the hen for a few more days.

Above: Temperature is one of the keys to successful hand-rearing. The formula must be the right temperature, and the chicks are kept warm in a brooder. Below: At six weeks of age, this Orange-chinned chick is being fed with an eyedropper. Facing page: A young Orange-chin, just weaned. Note that in this species the beak does not darken.

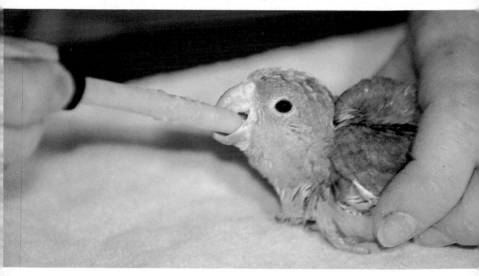

Hand-rearing   Anyone who has birds set up for breeding should always be prepared to hand-rear chicks at anytime. When one breeds birds, problems can arise at any moment, and by being prepared in advance and acting quickly, you may save a young chick's life. There are numerous reasons why a chick may have to be hand-reared. The parents may abandon the eggs, so the chicks are dependent on humans for their well-being. I have always found it necessary to have an incubator or two on hand. A small incubator is just a trivial investment, well worth the money if just one or two chicks are hatched. The ones with the clear plastic domes are nice because you can easily observe the eggs and the thermometers. Also, the temperature in these incubators can be adjusted with just a touch of the dial; thus, a lower temperature setting enables the incubator also to be used as a brooder for a very young chick. Eggs that are in an incubator must be turned at least three times a day. When the eggs are under the hen, she rotates them many times a day. This is done so the embryo will develop properly. If an egg is not turned often enough in each and every twenty-four-hour period, the chick could be born with leg disorders or it could be in the wrong position in the shell, making hatching impossible. The more an egg is turned, up to six times in a twenty-four-hour period, the better it is for the embryo. Hatching begins when a small hole appears on the shell. Turn the egg so the hole is facing up. After this the egg should no longer be turned. If your incubator has an automatic turner, shut it off, place the egg on a tray, or move the egg to another incubator without a turner.

We have two incubators set up at all times. The Marsh Farms Roll-X is set at 99.6 °F., with the wet bulb reading about 85 °F. A Marsh Farms Turn-X is set up for eggs that are starting to pip: 99 °F. dry bulb, with the wet-bulb thermometer at 95 °F. A higher humidity is needed for the pipping eggs, so they will remain moist. If it is too dry, the chick could become trapped inside the shell and die; in this case the chick would need help in hatching.

An incubator can also come in very handy for quickly warming up a cold chick that the parents have abandoned. Sometimes the parents get off the chicks for one reason or another. If they leave them unattended for too long, the chicks will become chilled. If the cold chicks are put in a set-up incubator, they will warm up instantly and usually turn out just fine. If you find a chick that is cold and appears to be dead, check it over thoroughly before tossing it out. I have found on occasion that a chick has crawled away from its nestmates, ending up in a corner of the nest box. After a close examination it was apparent that the chick was still alive and breathing, barely. The heated incubator warmed the chick back to life.

Another reason for pulling the chicks for hand-rearing would be the parents plucking their babies' feathers, causing the chicks to bleed. If these chicks are left in the nest box, they could end up being killed by the parents. This plucking could be caused by an insufficient diet, or possibly the pair want to return to nest. Some people hand-feed their chicks to increase production or to produce a very tame and lovable pet.

Whatever the reason for hand-rearing, be prepared to devote a lot of time and patience to this most satisfying task. It is indeed time consuming and may even be totally exhausting at times. A newly hatched chick must be fed every two hours around the clock, day and night, for the first week of life. But it is a very rewarding experience to see a beautiful, tame, feathered bird learning to eat seeds on its own, knowing that you put all that love and time into its care.

A few items should be kept on hand in case you have to hand-rear a chick unexpectedly. These would be an electric heating pad and a small cardboard box or a five-gallon

121

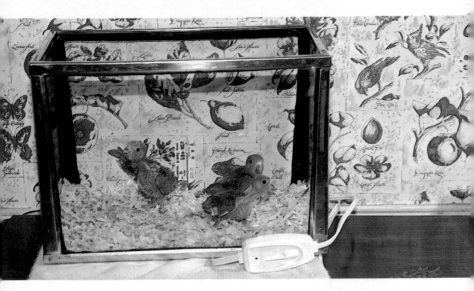

Above: A five-gallon aquarium can easily be turned into a brooder for chicks that are being hand-reared. Facing page: Corky, shown here at seven weeks of age, while being reared by hand. Below: Weighing chicks during hand-rearing can be very helpful, as most problems quickly show up as no gain or a loss in weight.

aquarium; a small eyedropper and a jar of Gerber baby food, Rice Cereal with Applesauce and Bananas. A cardboard box or glass aquarium is what I use as a brooder; either will do quite well. If you use a cardboard box, be sure it is clean and free of any odor. Once the babies are grown and transferred to a cage, the box is tossed out into the garbage, not reused for another brood of chicks. This arrangement is sanitary and prevents the spread of germs from brood to brood. If you have chicks set up in separate brooders, use separate eyedroppers and feeding utensils (bowls and spoons) for each group. Wash your hands before you handle babies from different brooders, as a precaution to help keep any disease from spreading.

Some people use a wooden box outfitted with a heating element and a thermostat. A wooden brooder box is adequate, but I feel that it is extremely difficult to thoroughly clean and sterilize wood. Glass aquariums have advantages which I particularly like. I can observe the chicks and the thermometer at all times through the clear, clean glass of the aquarium. Once the chicks are placed in a cage for weaning, the aquarium is soaked in a disinfectant and washed and dried out thoroughly.

I prepare a box or aquarium for use as a brooder by lining the bottom with paper toweling. I then add a one-inch layer of pine shavings on the bottom. The shavings will give the chicks a stable footing so spraddle leg will not develop. (In spraddle leg the legs do not develop properly, and the hip joints are weak, so the legs turn out to the sides.) If the shavings become too damp and soiled, they should be cleaned out and replaced with new shavings. After the box is prepared, the heating pad is then wrapped once around with a small bath towel. For a newly hatched chick, the entire box should be placed on top of the wrapped heating pad. For older chicks, three quarters of the box should be over the heating pad; this way, the chicks can move off the heated part of the box if

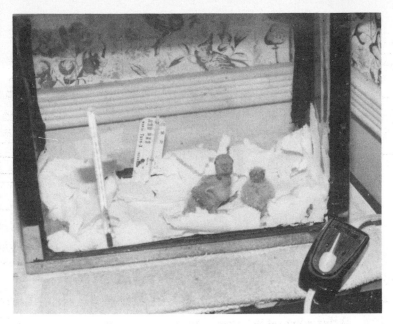

With two thermometers, the temperature in this brooder can be closely monitored. When chicks are this young, the right temperature is crucial to their well-being.

they become too warm. If the chicks want more heat, they will move some of the shavings and lie nearer the bottom of the box, where the heat comes through. The heating pad is set on the Medium setting. The box is then covered with a heavy towel, leaving about an inch open for fresh air. The towel will help to hold in the heat and can also be used to regulate the heat somewhat by varying the opening, but it must always be open a little for ventilation. If you find the chicks sitting up and panting, they are being kept too warm, so the heat in the brooder must be reduced till the babies are comfortable. The heat can be lowered by changing the setting to Low, wrapping the heating pad with another layer of towel, moving the box half way off the pad, or uncovering more

Above: Corky, the first Cobalt-winged Parakeet bred in the U.S., weighed 33 grams at 19 days of age, when a dated closed band was placed on his leg so that he could grow into it. Below: Corky at 30 days.

Above: In the following week, Corky's wing feathers grew rapidly. Below: At 49 days, with cobalt blue wing feathers nearly fully developed, Corky had already started to eat bread and was transferred from the brooder to a cage.

of the top. The bottom of the box should feel warm to the touch. If the chicks feel cool to the touch, the heat should be raised a little till the babies feel slightly warm.

I have a couple of thermometers in the brooder to keep track of the temperature at all times. One is placed directly on the floor to read the highest temperature. Another is taped at the level of the layer of shavings to get the cooler reading. Chicks up to ten days old are kept at a high-temperature reading of about 95°F., and those ten days to four weeks old are kept at about 85°F. When I have two or more four-week-old chicks in the brooder and the temperature in my house does not drop below 70°F., the heating pad is turned off during the day and turned back on toward evening. If there is only one chick by itself, the heating pad should not be shut off until almost all its feathers are completely grown in. As its feathers grow in, the pad can be set to Low during the day. When the chicks become fully feathered, they will no longer need any heat to keep them warm. At about five to six weeks old, they will be completely feathered and ready for a cage.

It is a good idea to have a gram scale on hand. This way, chicks can be weighed every day or two to be sure they are growing and gaining weight. The weight should be written down for future reference in case it is needed for comparison with another chick's weight. When you handle and feed a chick many times a day, sometimes it is difficult to tell whether the chick is gaining weight. By weighing the chick and keeping a log of the daily weight, you will know if everything is fine; if a problem is developing, it will show up as no weight gain or a loss of weight. Some chicks may cease to gain weight just before fledging age (five weeks old). They are losing their "baby fat" so they will be able to fly. At this time many start to cut back on the amount of food they will accept from the hand, as they start to sample soft food themselves.

Formula and Feeding Schedule The hand-rearing formula I use is given to the chicks from four days of age up through weaning. A large amount is made up in advance, of which a small portion is put in the refrigerator, while the remainder is packed in small plastic containers and stored in the freezer till needed. My formula can be kept refrigerated for five days and frozen for six months.

The following lists the ingredients and tells how I prepare the formula.

> 5 cups water
> 1 cup quick oatmeal
> ½ cup Wheat Hearts cereal
> ½ cup high-protein baby cereal
> ½ teaspoon salt
> 1 tablespoon corn oil
> 1 tablespoon honey (optional)

Starting with cold water, I add the salt, oil, and honey. Then I slowly add the dry cereals, stirring continuously to prevent lumping. After the cereal has cooked completely (three to five minutes after it boils), I remove the pot from the stove and add the following ingredients, stirring till they are well incorporated:

> 1 jar (4½ oz.) creamed spinach baby food
> 1 jar (4½ oz.) strained peas baby food
> 1 jar (4½ oz.) strained carrots baby food
> 1 jar (4½ oz.) creamed corn baby food
> 1 jar (4½ oz.) applesauce baby food
> 1 jar (4½ oz.) banana baby food
> ½ cup corn meal (optional)
> 1 cup powdered milk
> 2 cups sunflower meal

You can prepare your own sunflower meal or purchase it at a health-food store. To make your own, put sunflower kernels into a blender along with two slices of dried wheat bread broken up into crumbs, and blend till very fine. You may have to put in small amounts at a time, so it will be ground better, into a very fine powder. The dried bread crumbs keep the sunflower kernels from becoming sticky.

Once the formula is prepared, it must be put into small plastic containers and placed immediately in the refrigerator or freezer. If left out too long, bacteria could grow and cause serious problems when the chicks are fed. When the container I'm using starts to run low, another is taken out from the freezer and placed in the refrigerator to thaw. Keep in mind that it takes hours for the formula to become soft enough that it can easily be spooned out. I spoon out the amount I estimate will be needed for each feeding. After the chicks are all fed, any left-over formula is discarded. This formula may have to be thinned down with some water before feeding. It should be a very thin mush, a little thicker than a cream soup. I now warm the formula in a microwave oven, but for years I used a small pot on the stove. Stir the formula very well before feeding it to the chicks, because any hot spots in the formula could burn the chicks' throats. I test the formula on my upper lip. If it feels warm, not hot (100–101°F.), it is then fed to the chicks immediately, before it cools.

If the food is too cool, the chicks may be unable to digest it and could develop what is known as sour, or impacted, crop. The crop will not empty because the chick is not digesting the food and is in fact slowly starving. Sometimes a drop or two of blackstrap molasses or a pinch of baking soda added to some very thin (watered down) warm formula can help to relieve this problem. The crop should be massaged gently at each feeding till all the undigested food is gone. If the problem does not clear up in twenty-four hours, the crop should be cleaned out. To a half cup of warm water, add ¼ teaspoon of baking soda and stir well. With an eyedropper, feed a small amount of this mixture to the chick. Massage the crop very gently for a few seconds till it feels soft. Holding the chick with one hand, gently use the right thumb and index finger of the other to force the contents of the crop up and out of the mouth. You may have to hold the chick head down to do this. It must be done quickly to prevent choking. Do not worry if the crop does not get emptied out completely. Most of the time, the little bit that may be left will be digested by the chick. After the crop cleaning, feed the chick a very small amount of thin, warm, watery formula. The crop may have to be cleaned out one more time if too much soured food has stayed in the crop and has not been digested in a few hours. Just remember that it is much easier to prevent sour crop than to cure it!

Some chicks fed from day one will not always develop the "friendly bacteria" needed to break down food in the digestive tract. In such a case the chick may just stop digesting its food. This usually happens at about seven days of age. To prevent this problem I feed yogurt to furnish the needed bacteria. Instead of yogurt, a pinch of powdered acidophilus or a drop or two of the liquid form could be added to a few of the feedings—the result is the same. This is done first at about five days of age, and repeated again at ten days and at fifteen days. If a chick has been fed by the parents for even a couple of days, more than likely the parents have already passed on the bacteria needed for digestion, in the food regurgitated to their chicks.

For the first three days of a chick's life, each feeding should consist of only a couple of drops, by eyedropper, of Gerber Rice Cereal with Applesauce and Bananas. A very small amount is thinned down with water to make it into a very thin gruel, then warmed. At four days of age a very small amount of my formula is added to the Rice Cereal. During the next couple of days the amount of formula added is increased, till by the end of a week the chick is being fed straight formula. The chick is fed every two hours throughout the day during the first week. From seven to fourteen days old, the chick should be fed about every three hours during the day, every four hours at night, depending on how fast the chick digests the formula. From two to four weeks old, it should be fed four or five times a day, again depending on how fast the crop empties. From four weeks to six weeks of age, reduce the feedings to three or four times a day. Once the chick is fully feathered and placed in a cage, three feedings a day should be sufficient. When the young bird starts to sample food, two feedings a day will do until it is weaned.

I will admit that it is very difficult to say precisely how many feedings a day a chick should have. Each and every chick is different, just as each and every person hand-feeds differently. Some people prefer to feed less food at each meal, while others practically stuff their chicks to the brim. I have always found it best not to overfill a chick, and to feed a little more frequently. This usually helps to prevent impacted crop, while overfeeding a chick can cause crop and digestion difficulties sooner or later.

The foods first offered to promote self-feeding should be bread, apple, bananas, peas, corn, and water, soon followed by Budgerigar mix, sunflower seed, and safflower seed. Once the chick is eating fairly well on its own, you should still hand-feed it once in the evening before bedtime. This will ensure that the chick has enough food to get it through the night. If the chick refuses to be hand-fed, you should feel the crop. If the crop feels full, then the chick has probably eaten enough. Be sure to check the chick daily for a week to be sure it continues to eat well on its own before deciding that the chick is completely self-sufficient.

There are many other hand-rearing formulas that are currently being used with great success. I know of many people who are feeding a mixture of Purina Monkey Chow or Zu Preen Primate Dry and powdered milk. The monkey-chow biscuits are broken into small pieces and then put into a blender and ground to a fine powder. The powdered monkey chow is stored dry in a tightly sealed container. At each feeding, a small amount of the powdered monkey chow and some powdered milk are put into a bowl. The powdered milk adds calcium, which is needed if the chick is to grow properly. Hot water is added to the mixture, which is stirred well, till it becomes a smooth, thin gruel. As with any formula, it is tested just before being fed to the chick to make sure it is the proper temperature. After the chick is fed, any left-over formula is discarded. I have heard many excellent reports about this much less complex formula.

Many people develop their own formulas and techniques to hand-rear their chicks. I personally prefer to use an eyedropper, because it is less messy and I have more control over how much food is fed. The chick's mouth and beak must be cleaned thoroughly right after each feeding, or deformities of the mouth or beak could develop. You should use whatever hand-feeding tool is most comfortable for you and your chick. With patience and proper care you should end up with a healthy baby.

Problems in Breeding One always has the hope that in breeding birds everything will go well, but unfortunately this is not always the case. All we can do is provide everything that seems necessary and hope that nature will do its part. We should give breeding pairs as much privacy as possible, but at the same time keep a close watch for any complications that may arise. This way, one can step right in and give a helping hand, if possible. For example, when a pair of birds are starting to show signs of nesting, the hen should be watched carefully to make sure she does not become egg bound.

There are many reasons why eggs do not hatch. The most common is that the egg was not fertile, perhaps because the pair did not copulate, or the male simply may be too young. There is always a slim chance that the male is sterile. Sometimes a well-balanced diet high in vitamin E will correct these problems.

There are also many reasons why fertile eggs do not hatch. If an entire clutch of fertile eggs do not hatch, maybe sometime during incubation the pair left the eggs for too long. Sometimes birds are frightened off the nest during the night by such things as thunder storms, cats and rodents roaming about, and dogs barking. The pair may not be able to find their way back to the nest box until dawn. You would have no idea that there had been a problem in the middle of the night. Unfortunately, if fertile eggs are left unattended for long on a cold night, by morning the embryos inside may be dead. The pair may continue to incubate these eggs, but none will hatch.

A clutch may not hatch because of inconsistent incubation. There may have been distractions in the vicinity, causing the pair to leave the nest box too often, out of sheer curiosity. Also, a pair may simply be too young, and not yet ready to settle down to raise a family.

If none of the eggs of successive clutches hatch or if the chicks die soon afterwards, there may be a bacterial problem. It would be advisable to have a vet run cultures on both parents and even the unhatched, dead eggs. One bird or both could be harboring some sort of infection that is transmitted to the eggs, causing the embryos to die. Or the chicks may die soon after hatching, even though they are being fed and cared for well by their parents. If the cultures come back positive, your vet will prescribe the proper medicine. Once the problem has been corrected, fertile eggs soon should be turning into beautiful healthy birds.

If an embryo dies before hatching, it is possible that the shell could have had a hairline fracture or was too porous. Such eggs can become infected with germs, or they may simply dry up.

During the hot summer months the nest can become too dry. The birds must be supplied with fresh water for bathing, so they can keep the eggs moist. If the eggs become too dry, the chicks will not be able to break through the hard shell or even the tough inner membrane. There are times when nothing can be done to prevent these heartaches. We had a pair of Grey-cheeked Parakeets sitting on four eggs, all fertile. About a week before the eggs were due to hatch, we were hit with a heat wave. The temperature rose to 110°F. in the shade. The nest box was well shaded, and the birds would bathe to wet the eggs and cool them off. But the high temperature just cooked the eggs and, as you can guess, they never hatched.

After the first pip, a chick can take up to forty-eight hours to emerge from the egg. In the last few hours the tiny chick is taking in the last of the yolk sac which fed the chick until it was time to hatch. Once the yolk sac is completely inside, the chick will hatch. A chick normally starts to pip at the larger end of the egg shell, using the egg tooth that is on the tip of the upper mandible. There are times when a chick is in the wrong position in the egg. Instead of pipping around the large end of the egg, they pip on the smaller end. Some of these chicks can pip out on their own; others end up drowning in their own fluids. If the chick is in the wrong position and the shell has been pipped thirty-six to forty-eight hours, the chick may be helped out, slowly and gently. It could happen that the membrane in the shell dried out too much and stuck to the chick, preventing it from freeing itself from the shell.

If you know that a chick is trapped inside the shell, you can try to help it out. With a toothpick, very carefully pick off bits of the end of the shell where the chick has fractured the egg. If any bleeding should occur, you must stop and try again later. In the meantime, put the egg in an incubator. If the chick bleeds a lot, dab on some styptic powder, or even flour, to stop the bleeding before placing the egg in the incubator.

As you pick off tiny pieces of shell, watch where the chick is inside. Be very careful not to poke the chick with the toothpick. Do not take off pieces of the egg shell below where the chick has been breaking through. If the membrane is dry and hard, you can dampen it with a slightly wet cotton swab. Do not get any moisture on the chick's face, or it may drown. After the chick's face is clear and it can breathe, place the egg in an incubator to see if the chick can hatch out the rest of the way on its own. If the chick still has not hatched after a few hours, try taking off more of the shell around the chick's head. Soon the baby will emerge. Once it has hatched, it can be returned to the parents. If it is going to be hand-reared, the incubator temperature should be lowered to about 96 °F. The first feeding should be given between two and four hours after the time of hatching.

Just remember that not every egg will hatch. Even with birds living in their natural environment not all the eggs of every clutch hatch. Just be sure your birds are receiving a well-balanced diet that is high in calcium, so the egg shells will be strong. Improper nutrition may result in a weak chick that will be unable to hatch or is deformed. We can only do our best, and then let nature take its course, possibly with a little help from us.

Health Tips

Veterinary Help   Birds have become very popular in the past decade, not only as pets. Many people are also devoting much time to the hobby of breeding birds. With all this interest in birds, more and more veterinarians are starting to specialize in their treatment. If you do not know of a vet who specializes in birds, you should locate one. There are various ways to find a good bird vet. Pet shops that carry a good selection of birds usually can recommend one. You can also try contacting local bird breeders or bird clubs. Vets who do not specialize in birds often know one who does.

Sometimes, when problems arise, it is possible to treat your own bird. But there are other times when veterinary help is a necessity. I have found it extremely important to be in touch with a good bird veterinarian at all times, in case of an emergency. There are situations when only the combined knowledge and experience of a good bird vet can save a bird's life!

A vet can perform many services, depending on what needs to be done. If you have just purchased a new bird and all you want is the vet's opinion about the health of the bird, then a visual checkup may be all that's needed. The vet will check the skin, feathers, vent area, eyes, throat, tongue, mouth, and body weight. If you want the beak and claws clipped, or the wings trimmed, your vet can do this easily. If the bird is ill or the vet suspects a problem, other tests may be needed. Throat and fecal cultures can determine whether the bird has a bacterial infection. Not only will the vet know from the tests which illness he is dealing with, he'll also know what kind of medicine will remedy the problem. A test of the bird's droppings can also show if any internal parasites are present. Blood tests may also be needed. A blood test could show a high white-corpuscle count, for example, which could mean the bird is harboring a bacterial or viral infection. We have always found that blood tests combined with cultures are very successful in diagnosing a bird's problem. Taking blood for testing is a very simple procedure for a vet to perform. One claw is cut to the quick, and a very small amount of blood is drawn into a special, thin glass tube. Usually, by the time the vet has enough blood for testing (it takes less than a minute) the bleeding has already stopped. If not, a little styptic powder is applied to the cut claw, and the bleeding stops immediately.

A vet can also set and cast broken legs and mend fractured wings. Tumors can be removed surgically by an experienced vet. Our vet cured a case of poisoning by giving an injection combined with oral medication; the next day our bird was fine and ready to come home.

Should you ever come across any questionable situations, it is always best to contact your vet for his expert advice. Your vet can be your bird's best friend. If your bird is injured or becomes ill, a prompt visit to the vet could save the bird's life.

First Aid   If a bird is not feeling well, it will usually not be as active as it is normally. Many ill birds will cut back on their food intake and sit with their feathers puffed up, usually sleeping a lot. As the bird's condition deteriorates, its eyes will appear dull, its droppings will usually become watery, and it will rapidly lose weight. If it has an upper respiratory illness, discharge from the nostrils may be seen. It is best not to let the bird's condition worsen, as this only makes it more difficult to cure the illness.

At the very first sign of any abnormality, the bird

should be put on heat. If you don't have a hospital cage, a small cage placed on a heating pad turned to the Medium setting will do. Cover the top of the cage and three sides with a heavy bath towel or blanket, leaving most of the front open for air. This will help to keep most of the warmth inside the cage. Touch the floor of the cage to be sure it is warm, but not overly hot. A thermometer placed on the front of the cage close to the bottom can help you regulate the temperature, which should be between 85 and 90 °F. Offer the bird plenty of food (seed and soft food), along with fresh water, so it will continue to eat and drink. A bird being kept warm will drink more water than usual so it will not dehydrate.

If the bird does not appear to improve in about twenty-four hours, the bird should be taken to a vet. The bird could have a bacterial or a viral infection which must be treated. A throat culture might be taken to determine what the problem is. If you have given any antibiotics to a bird before a culture is taken, it may kill enough of the bacteria to cause a negative result, even if the antibiotic is the wrong type for this particular problem. The antibiotic may diminish the infection but not cure it totally. After the culture results are in (which takes twenty-four to forty-eight hours), the vet will know exactly which antibiotic is needed for the illness, but meanwhile he may start the bird on a broad-spectrum antibiotic immediately.

If there is no chance of a vet seeing your bird, you can start the bird on one of the remedies that can be purchased at a pet store. Without proper testing it is very difficult to diagnose what ails a bird, so you should administer a broad-spectrum antibiotic. It should be used as directed on the label. Different antibiotics should not be used at the same time unless a vet directs you to do so. These antibiotics can be administered to the bird in the drinking water or given orally, depending on what is recommended on the package or the recommendation of a vet. Normally a bird treated orally (by eyedropper or syringe) responds more quickly to the medicine for, as my vet always says, "When you put the medicine in the water, all you treat is the water." Many birds can go without water for days at a time. If they do not like the taste of the medicated water, they simply will not drink any, or very little, and not get enough of the medicine to cure the problem.

Preventing Illness   Keep in mind that preventing a disease is far easier than curing one. The cleanliness of a bird's cage is very important, as well as where it is located.

When you keep a bird in the house, remember that it has no resistance to drafts and sudden changes in the surrounding temperature. The average house pet does not have an adequate undercoat of downy feathers to protect it from a sudden drop in temperature, such as an outdoor aviary bird has developed. It is extremely important to protect your pet from drafts of any kind. Excess heat also can cause problems for your bird, such as causing a year-around molt that would lower a bird's resistance to disease and promote an illness.

Brotogeris parakeets can live to be fifteen years old, or even older, provided they are fed and cared for properly. Many pet owners actually kill their birds with kindness by feeding unsuitable foods or allowing their pets to wander about the house eating food from people's plates. Many kinds of food we eat, such as oily fried foods and sweets, can harm a bird. Use common sense when allowing your pet to sample foods. If you do use common sense, feed a proper diet, and offer fresh, clean water, your pet should stay healthy and live a long life, with few problems.

Accidents and Injuries   Some bird owners let their pets have freedom of the house without any supervision. Many of these birds are severely hurt or killed. I know of many cases of pet birds that have been stepped on and even sat upon. I even heard a very sad story about a young person who was confined to a wheelchair. Someone in the household let his bird out of its cage for exercise. The bird, being very attached to its young owner, decided to go roaming about the house to seek him out. As the young boy came down a hallway in his wheelchair, he did not notice his little feathered friend was coming up the other way, looking for him. It was very unfortunate that he accidentally ran over the bird.

There are many things in the home that can injure a pet bird. Be sure fans are turned off while your pet is let out of its cage. Many of these loose birds end up escaping through windows or doors which had been left open. Most escaped pet birds are rarely recovered by their owners. If someone else doesn't find these birds and keep them, most die of hunger or are attacked by wild birds and animals. I have also heard of dogs, cats, ferrets, and even a pet snake that did in the family's flighted pet bird.

Fully flighted pet birds that are let out of their cages for exercise can be spooked and fly headfirst into a window or mirror. If the bird knocks itself out, place the bird in a cage and keep it quiet and warm. If the bird does not return to normal within an hour, it should be examined by a vet.

If a bird fractures a leg or a wing, it should be taken to a vet so the fracture can be set properly. A wing fracture that is not set properly will usually result in a droopy, hanging wing for life, and the bird may never be able to fly again. A broken leg that is not set correctly can end up swollen and painful, making it difficult for the bird to walk and perch. It may even be unable to hold certain foods to eat. Fractures normally heal within two to three weeks. Your vet may instruct you to remove all perches except one close to the floor of the cage. Food and water dishes should be placed on the floor too. This will keep the bird quiet and discourage it from climbing about the cage. It is probably best not to play with the bird during this crucial healing time.

If you find your pet holding one leg up and not putting any weight on it, this does not necessarily mean the leg is broken. The bird may have simply hurt or sprained its leg. The treatment is the same as if the bird had broken its leg. Keep the bird quiet, remove all perches but one, and place feed and water cups on the floor of the cage. Usually, within ten days the bird will regain the use of its leg, when the muscles or joints have healed.

If a bird is injured by another bird, they must be separated immediately. If the injury is very minor, medication may not be necessary. But should the bird be severely injured and bleeding, first aid will be required. The wounds should be cleaned with hydrogen peroxide to help the body fight off any infection. A topical antibiotic such as Terramycin Ophthalmic Ointment can be applied to the injured areas. The injured bird should be kept warm in a hospital cage till it feels better. The bird should not be returned to a cage with other birds till its wounds have healed completely.

The chance that a bird can have a mishap is sometimes quite high. There are many kinds of accidents that can happen to a bird, so all we can do is to keep an eye on our pet, and to use good judgment especially when it is allowed out of its cage.

Overgrown Beaks   Parrots flying free in the wild constantly use their beaks for climbing as well as for chewing on various things. These birds enjoy gnawing on wood and branches, as chewing helps to keep their beaks trim and worn down, preventing them from becoming overgrown. *Brotogeris* parakeets will gnaw on wood, but they are not as destructive as other parrots, such as conures and macaws. Overgrown beak problems are more common with pets caged indoors than with

142

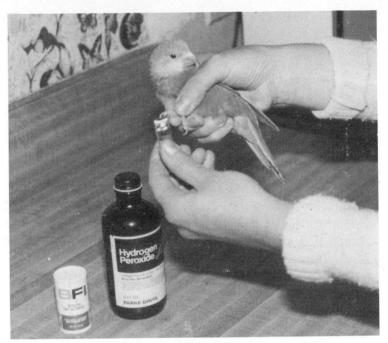

Clipping a Grey-cheek's claws with a fingernail clipper. Always be prepared in case of bleeding.

birds in an outdoor aviary. This is usually the case because the indoor bird has little to chew on to keep its beak worn down, but sometimes this problem is caused by a beak or jaw deformity. A jaw disorder is usually permanent and cannot be corrected, so beak trimming will be necessary whenever the beak becomes overgrown. Whatever the cause, the overgrown beak must be trimmed, otherwise it could hamper eating. A bird with a badly overgrown beak might also get its beak caught in something and injure itself.

Beak trimming can be done by a vet, or you can do it yourself. If you prefer to trim the beak yourself, you can use a fingernail clipper. Only very tiny pieces should be cut at a time, so you do not cut into the quick, till the desired length and shape is attained. Should the beak start to bleed, apply a styptic powder to stop the bleeding. Hydrogen peroxide and flour will do the trick if nothing else is handy at the time. If the beak starts to bleed before enough has been taken off, discontinue the trimming and try later on that day or the next. Do not trim a beak just to dull the sharp point. This tip enables the bird to crack and eat seed. Trim the beak only if it has grown far beyond its normal length.

Cauterizers suitable for use on birds are now being sold by some suppliers. Once, in the middle of the night, a young bird, almost weaned, somehow broke off the tip of its upper mandible. Thank goodness I was up at that time to feed some chicks. I tried some styptic powder, but it would not stop the blood, which was actually dripping from the broken beak. The only other thing I could think of was to cauterize it. I grabbed a very old "It's a Boy" cigar, left over from when my son was born, and lit it up. There I was at two o'clock in the morning, learning how to smoke. I lightly pressed the lit cigar to the tip of the badly bleeding beak, and the bleeding stopped instantly.

Claw Trimming   Quite often a bird's claws will become overgrown and need a bit of trimming. This is a much more common problem with house pets, but occasionally it does occur with aviary birds. I have found that using branches for perches instead of wooden dowels can help wear down the claws of most birds remarkably well. A bird's claws should be trimmed only when necessary. A fingernail clipper can be used on small parrots. Before you begin, hold the bird's foot up to a light to locate the small blood vessel that runs into the claw. Usually this blood vessel is easy to spot, and you'll want to avoid cutting into it when you are trimming. Claws cut too short can cause a bird much discomfort. It is easier if one person holds the bird while another does the clipping. The bird should be held firmly, as the slightest movement can cause you to cut off too much of the claw, and bleeding will result. If this happens, saturate a cotton ball in hydrogen peroxide and apply it to the bleeding claw. Usually the bleeding stops immediately. Styptic powders will also stop the bleeding, and these can be purchased at any drug store. If the bleeding is slight, baby powder or flour should work quite well.

If you do not wish to attempt claw trimming yourself, your vet will be very happy to, for a small fee. If you have never trimmed a bird's claws before, it would be wise to let your vet do it, at least the first time. Ask if you can watch while this procedure is being done, so you can do it yourself the next time it is necessary.

Mites   Several different kinds of mites can attack your bird if it is not cared for properly. The most common is the red mite. These are very tiny but can just be seen with the naked eye. They are red in color because of the blood they suck from their victims. If your bird has quite a few mites feeding on it, it can become anemic and pale in color, with resistance lowered, and vulnerable to diseases. If the mites are not taken care of, they can even cause the death of the bird. These mites live in the cracks and crevices of the bird cage and only crawl on the bird to feed, usually at night.

To prevent red mites, clean the cage thoroughly at least once a month. Remove the bird and food and water cups, and take the cage outside and spray it with a bird-mite spray. With outdoor aviaries, spray the corners, walls, shelves, and any place where mites could hide. Also, be sure to spray nest boxes after each brood of chicks have fledged. If the birds have not bred and produced chicks, spray the nest boxes every three months anyway. Again, it is very important to use only insecticides made for use on or around birds, and be sure to remove the food and water when spraying.

If you do not spray the aviaries and nest boxes periodically, you could end up losing chicks. I had a friend bring over a couple of Cockatiel chicks that were almost three weeks old. The chicks were in their nest box, and he asked me to try to save the babies, as the parents had chewed the chicks badly, making them bleed. As I lifted a very bloody chick out for inspection, I noticed that my hands and arms were covered with hundreds of tiny mites. I quickly took the chicks outside and sprayed myself and the babies with Hargate spray. It was now apparent that the parent birds were not attacking their young out of malice, but instead trying desperately to remove the mites that were killing their chicks. Needless to say, the chicks and I lived through this horrible experience, and the owner of the Cockatiels thoroughly sprayed his aviaries to rid the place of mites.

Feather mites also can be a problem. If a bird's feathers appear to be ragged and chewed up, even on the head where the bird cannot reach, and there are no other birds being kept in the same cage, it would be safe to assume that the bird has feather mites. This mite is found more often on outdoor aviary birds, but sometimes on house pets. If a bird has feather mites, the bird itself must be sprayed. Use only a spray that is for direct use on birds, or a spray your vet recommends. Lightly spray the bird's back, sides, wings, tail, and breast. With your finger, apply some of the spray to the sides and top of the head. Do this by spraying some of the spray on a paper towel or on your hand, but do not spray directly in the bird's face, as this could be harmful. Be very careful not to get spray in the bird's eyes. I have had very good results using Hargate spray for feather mites. Some vets eliminate feather mites with a special solution, dipping the bird's body only in the mixture, then applying it to the head

146

feathers, being very careful not to get it in the eyes, mouth, or nostrils. You can consult your vet for the best method for eliminating feather mites from your bird.

Never spray a room with insecticide while your bird is in it. Before you start to spray, remove both the bird and its cage to a different room and make sure the door is closed so no fumes from the spray will come in contact with the bird or its food. Do not return the cage and bird to the sprayed room for about five hours. Most insecticides are toxic to birds, but those using pyrethrins are generally safe. It is always wise to check with your vet before using any kind of insecticide on or around your bird.

Before using a No-Pest Strip in the same room with your bird, check with your vet. I personally do not like using these with my animals. These insect strips release a vapor of nerve poison continuously. Many contain a chemical that has the potential for doing some genetic damage, and no one knows for sure what other damage it can do over a long period.

Scaly-face and scaly-leg mites are common in some birds, but not in *Brotogeris* parakeets. These mites affect the bird's beak, cere, facial area, and legs. On the legs it causes abnormal-looking scales, and infested areas on the head appear dirty and crusty or sometimes look reddish and inflamed. An oily medicine called Scalex will clear up this condition and get rid of these mites. It can be applied with a cotton swab to the affected areas. The cage perches should also be rubbed down with Scalex to discourage the presence of these mites. Scalex will smother the mites, and if treated promptly, the bird will heal quickly and soon will look as good as new. Be sure to follow the directions that are on the bottle. Scalex is strictly for *external* use.

Worming   Birds kept as pets indoors normally do not have problems with worms. But keep in mind that there is always the possibility that a bird may have contracted these parasites before you got it. If a bird seems to be in good health but is slightly thin and eats quite a lot, there is a chance that the bird has worms. There are many different kinds of worms, but roundworms are the most common. If a bird with this problem is left untreated, it could become very weak and die. Your vet can run a quick and inexpensive lab test to see if the bird does have worms, and if so, exactly what kind of worms they are. Generally, a bird with worms is treated two or three times, at two-week intervals. This way, the worm eggs which could hatch after the first treatment will be taken care of. The exact medicine and treatment schedule will depend on your vet's findings.

If birds are being kept outdoors, it is fairly easy for them to get worms from the droppings of sparrows or other wild birds hopping along the top of the aviary, for example. As a precaution, my birds outdoors are wormed twice a year. I use Tramisol, mixing one teaspoon of Tramisol powder into three gallons of fresh, clean water. All the water bowls are cleaned out and refilled with the worming solution, so it is the only water available. This can be left before the birds for two days in cool weather, but only a day and a half in very warm weather. After the worming treatment the birds are put back on fresh drinking water. If you find that any of the birds do have worms (some birds will pass these organisms in their feces when they are put on the worming medicine), then this treatment should be repeated two more times, with two weeks between each treatment.

Before treating any bird for worms, it is best to discuss it with your vet.

Breeding the Cobalt-winged Parakeet

The little Cobalt-winged Parakeet (*Brotogeris cyanoptera cyanoptera*) was not common in private collections in the United States until just a few years ago. Back in September of 1981, we learned of a shipment of "Orange-chinned Parakeets" just released from quarantine. A few bird dealers noticed that these charming little birds resembled the Orange-chinned Parakeet but were in fact not that species. Their coloring was different; a yellow forehead and bright cobalt-blue wings were the most obvious differences. At that time, these extraordinary birds were being sold quite inexpensively, straight from the quarantine station, to bird jobbers and pet stores. Many bird dealers simply sold these unusual birds as pets, calling them "Orange-chinned Parakeets."

We were told that a local pet shop had some, so we immediately "flew" down to the shop. As Fred and I gazed upon these feathered creatures, we realized that these birds were not Orange-chinned Parakeets, but Cobalt-winged Parakeets. There were about twenty in the cage, and we decided to buy four birds, hoping to end up with at least one pair. Fred very carefully went through all of them, checking their pelvic bones, till he had four healthy birds which he strongly felt were two males and two females. Two had just slightly larger heads and beaks, and the other two had more delicate faces. We went home with our first Cobalt-winged Parakeets, the first we'd seen and also the first we'd owned.

The next day, I took the four birds to our veterinarian, Dr. Max E. Weiss, so he could sex them surgically for us. The four birds did indeed turn out to be two healthy pairs; the slightly larger ones were the males. The birds were tattooed on the undersides of the wings and marked with black ink on their feet—males on the right and hens left—for easy identification. I was so excited with our new birds that I went right home and set them up in a breeding cage. This was a long wire-mesh cage divided into two sections by a mesh partition. Fred went outside to check up on our new birds to see how they were doing. He quickly came back to the house to find out what new breeding technique I was trying. He admitted that the birds had been set up in a nice breeding cage, but suggested we would have much better luck producing chicks if I paired males with females instead of putting two males in one section and two hens in the other. I went out immediately and swapped the birds. To this day I don't know how I made this mistake. Could it have been all the excitement? I guess anyone can make a mistake, but just think how the birds must have felt.

The pairs were set up in this cage for well over a year with no sign of any attempts to breed. They were on what we believe to be an excellent diet, as all our birds receive this diet and are in good feather and fine health, and most produce chicks. I noticed that during the day the birds would hang on the mesh divider and try to preen each other's mates through the wire. As evening came, the pairs would retreat to their nest boxes for the night. It was early spring when we decided to try housing both pairs together in a larger cage. Two Budgerigar nest boxes (6 x 8 x 8 inches high), were hung on the outside of the cage. I read and talked to many people about Cobalt-wings and learned that in the wild they mostly nested in termite mounds. We decided to try something different with their nest boxes, so I lined the entire inside of the box with dark-colored cork wall paneling, using a nontoxic white glue to attach it to the inside walls. A small amount of pine shavings was placed inside.

As soon as the pairs were together in same cage, they swapped mates. It was now evident that they had not been happy with the way we had had them paired. Both pairs investigated both nest boxes, then decided to set up housekeeping together in the same nest box. Every evening, all four birds would climb into the nest box together. I peeked in there one day, just as it was getting dark, to see how they all did it. It was indeed crowded, but they all seemed happy and content. Two weeks after we put them all together, I noticed one of the hens starting to swell in the vent area. Soon the first egg was laid. Most of the cork in the nest box had been left intact; just a little had been chewed off and mixed in with the pine shavings. The hen had made a concave in one corner of the nest box for the egg. The laying hen incubated her egg, and her mate entered the nest box periodically during the day, probably to feed her. At dusk the future father, along with the other pair of Cobalt-winged Parakeets, joined the incubating hen to sleep for the night. I decided that four birds sleeping in one small nest box was too many, especially with one pair nesting. The next day I tried to remove the other pair, but this only upset the nesters. The male would call to the other birds, and the hen kept getting off her egg. Within an hour I returned the other pair to the cage. I was quite determined to raise a Cobalt-winged Parakeet, so I decided to remove the egg. Giving the hen an infertile Lineolated Parakeet egg in exchange for her egg, I placed it in our incubator. That night, as before, all four birds proceeded to sleep in the same nest box. The next morning, during my daily nest-box inspections, I found that the infertile Lineolated egg had been cracked.

The Cobalt-winged hen proceeded to lay a second egg, and soon she finished the clutch: a total of five eggs, laid every other day. Since I had one egg in the incubator, I decided to leave the remaining eggs with the hen till she was finished laying. About a week after I pulled the first egg, I took in the remaining four eggs and gave her more infertile eggs to incubate. I was just not comfortable with the idea of all four birds climbing into the same nest box each evening. I imagined finding scrambled eggs one morning, or the chicks could end up being smothered.

In a week we candled the eggs and discovered that three were clear. The first egg the hen laid was fertile, as was one of the remaining four eggs. We have a very good egg candler, and we could see that the second fertile egg had a problem. The embryo in this egg was developing in a sideways position, instead of being in the middle. I knew that this chick would more than likely need assistance at hatching time. All the eggs were about the same size: four measured 30/32 x 24/32 inches, and one was 30/32 x 25/32. These eggs were similar in size to Peach-faced Lovebird eggs.

The first chick hatched twenty-four days after the egg was placed in the incubator. Thirty-eight hours passed from the time of the first crack till the chick hatched out. Hatching began in our incubator, but just as the chick was ready to come out of the shell, it was placed under our very reliable Bourke's Parakeets. This pair had a few newly hatched chicks, as well as one egg soon to hatch. This pair of Bourke's have not only done a tremendous job rearing their own chicks, but they have fostered some Lineolated Parakeets and Cactus Conure chicks and done well with these too. Less than an hour after being placed in the Bourke's nest, the Cobalt-winged chick hatched. It was the size of a three-day-old Bourke's Parakeet chick, but with much less white down. The Bourke's pair immediately accepted their new arrival.

The next night (a Saturday), the second fertile Cobalt-winged egg started to hatch. I had calculated that hatching would not occur for another two days. On Monday morning the chick was still working on hatching, so I placed the egg under the Bourke's pair. By early afternoon, it was obvious that the second chick was growing weaker and could not free itself from the shell. I expected trouble, which is why I kept a close watch on this egg. I brought the egg back into the house and placed it in an incubator set up for hatching, with high humidity. I decided to very carefully chip some of the shell away from the chick's head so it could breathe. The chick had developed badly and was not in the correct position. The egg was put back into the incubator, and after a few hours I checked to see how the chick was doing. I could see there was yellow and white fluid building up in the egg. I felt it was finally time to extract the chick. With care I slowly chipped off the entire end of the egg and gently pulled the chick free. The chick was immediately put back in the incubator to warm up and dry off. In about three hours the chick was placed under the Bourke's Parakeets, and by evening it had been fed.

When the two chicks were eight and five days old, they were brought into the house for hand-rearing. The older chick weighed 15 grams, and the younger one 6 grams. The foster parents were doing a wonderful job feeding the Cobalt-winged chicks, but the second chick still appeared to be weak and very small. The older chick was more than twice its size. The younger chick ceased to grow and soon died, when eight days old.

The remaining chick grew rapidly. At twelve days of age, when his eyes opened, he weighed 18 grams. Even at this very young age, he had a loud and powerful voice, very similar to a Grey-cheeked Parakeet. At fourteen days, he weighed 25 grams, and dark feathers could be seen developing under the skin. This chick never developed a thick second down, unlike chicks of many other parrot species. When he was twenty-six days old and weighed about 40 grams, feathers started to "pop" through the sheaths on his tail and wings. At this point, the Cobalt-winged chick greatly resembled a Rose-ringed Parakeet chick because of the longish neck and "leggy" appearance but, of course, was much smaller in size. His feet were a very light gray. The upper mandible was two-toned, a dark gray color just below the cere and pink towards the tip. The lower mandible was pink. By six weeks of age the chick was just about completely feathered, and he was placed in a cage. At seven weeks old he was eating soft foods and some seed, Budgerigar mix being his favorite. The chick looked very much like his parents, the most noticeable difference being the beak color, almost black at the base of the upper mandible. His plumage color was not as bright as the adults'. This chick was just so sweet that we decided to keep him as a house pet. We named him Corky, and he is doing just great! He is now 61 grams, totally independent, and spoiled rotten, but simply adorable!

Recently, we had what almost turned out to be a tragic catastrophe with Corky. It was late evening when my son, Larry, noticed that Corky was not being his perky self. Earlier that day he was fine and had been eating well. All of a sudden, he seemed extremely weak, off-balance, and very unsteady on his feet. Corky was placed in a hospital cage to keep him warm and quiet, to prevent him from going into shock. That it was a holiday week-end only made matters worse when it came to finding a good veterinarian. Poor Corky started periodically to have what appeared to be seizures. Once, as he fell over on his side, I even thought he had died. Then he pulled himself up on his feet. Of course by now he was no longer eating or drinking, so I started to force-feed him gently. Remarkably, he remembered being hand-fed as a chick, so he took to the eyedropper easily. After two days of this ordeal to keep him alive, we were able to take him to Dr. Hannis Stoddard.

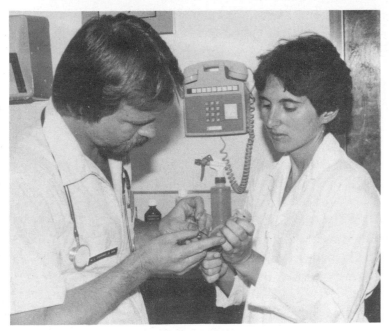

Dr. Hannis L. Stoddard III and his assistant, Tracy, taking blood from a Grey-cheek for testing.

Dr. Stoddard immediately ran all sorts of tests, which only showed how bad Corky's health was by now. No bacteria or virus was detected on these tests, and Corky was much too weak to withstand an X-ray. We all agreed that it must have been poisoning. With Dr. Stoddard's quick work, Corky started to improve at least enough to take an X-ray. The X-ray showed that something—maybe paint—was in his system. There was such a small amount by then that it was hard to identify, as the medicine already given for a toxic substance was doing its job.

For days we all tried to figure out what Corky could have gotten hold of and eaten. About a week later we heard a warning that some new "opaque outlining marker pens" were toxic and should be used with care. It just so happened that I had bought some of these fancy marking pens for my son. Nowhere on the pens was there anything about toxicity. The ink had a very strong smell, and one pen started to leak as Larry wrote with it. The ink got on his fingers and proved very difficult to remove. We now think that Corky may have chewed some paper with this ink on it, or maybe got some from Larry's hand. Whatever the cause, we now know that one can never be too careful. Thanks to Dr. Stoddard's quick work, Corky recovered totally in about two weeks. I am happy to say he is fine and happy, and shows no side effects from this ordeal. He is being watched like a hawk to be sure he doesn't get into anything else that could possibly hurt him.

*Fred and Robbie Harris received a 1983 Avy Award
from the American Federation of Aviculture
for the first breeding of the Cobalt-winged Parakeet
in the United States.*

Bibliography

Arrowood, Patricia C. 1980. Importation and status of Canary-winged Parakeets (*Brotogeris versicolorus* P. L. S. Muller) in California. In *Conservation of New World Parrots*, ed. R. F. Pasquier. Washington: Smithsonian Inst. Press.

Bates, Henry J., and Busenbark, Robert L. 1979. *Parrots and Related Birds*. 3rd ed. Neptune, NJ: T.F.H. Publications.

Forshaw, Joseph M. 1977. *Parrots of the World*. Neptune, NJ: T.F.H. Publications.

Gray, Annie P. 1958. *Bird Hybrids*. Farnham Royal, Bucks.: Commonwealth Agricultural Bureaux.

Harris, Robbie. 1983. *Breeding Conures*. Neptune, NJ: T.F.H. Publications.

Low, Rosemary. 1972. *The Parrots of South America*. London: John Gifford.

———. 1980. *Parrots, Their Care and Breeding*. Poole, Dorset: Blandford Press.

Peters, James Lee. 1937. *A Check-list of Birds of the World*. Vol. 3. Cambridge, MA: Harvard University Press.

Ridgely, Robert S. 1980. The current distribution and status of mainland neotropical parrots. In *Conservation of New World Parrots*, ed. by R. F. Pasquier. Washington: Smithsonian Inst. Press.

Rutgers, A., and Norris, K. A., eds. 1972. *Encyclopaedia of aviculture*. Vol. 2. London: Blandford Press.

Seth-Smith, David. 1979. *Small Parrots (Parrakeets)*. Neptune, NJ: T.F.H. Publications.

A Grey-cheeked Parakeet grooming its foot.

Index

References in boldface indicate
illustrations.